궁
정
비
사

宮闕秘史

궁궐비사

저자 : 고경아
편집 : 고수현

출판사 : 황금시대
출판등록 : 2016년 12월 08일 (제2016-000372호)
공식스토어 : 프라임뮤즈
대표전화 : 070. 7764. 7070
자격증문의 : 010. 7141. 8794

ISBN : 979-11-966111-5-6
ISBN : 979-11-966111-6-3

판매 및 리셀러 문의 : 070-7764-7070

Secret of the Kingdom

Author : Kyoung-A Ko
Director : Su-Hyun Ko

Publishing Company : Golden Age
Store : www.primemuse.com
Instagram : www.instagram.com/prime_muse
E-mail : support@primemuse.com

ISBN : 979-11-966111-5-6
ISBN : 979-11-966111-6-3

Wholesale and Retail Inquiries
support@primemuse.com

타로심리상담사란?

타로카드와 상담을 활용하여 피상담자의 현상 또는 심리상태에 대해 파악하고 구체적인 해결방안을 제시하여 피상담자의 문제해결을 도우며, 교육대상자에 대하여 타로카드를 활용한 소통, 심리 안정, 잠재능력의 발현 등 체계적이고 전문적인 교육 서비스를 제공하는 직무를 수행합니다.

자격증 특징

[타로심리상담사]는 프라임뮤즈에서 발행된 타로카드 기반으로 이루어진 자격증입니다. 만신/궁궐비사 등 앞으로 계속해서 출시될 많은 타로카드를 비롯하여, 내가 원하는 카드를 배울 수 있고, 원저작자의 의도를 한눈에 파악하여 누구보다 쉽게 이해함으로써 실전상담에 바로 적용하실 수 있습니다.

또한 필요에따라 유니버셜웨이트 / 올드잉글리쉬와 같은 가장 기본이 되는 타로카드 교육도 받으실 수 있습니다.

타로심리상담사 자격증 종류

타로심리상담사 1급
타로심리상담사 2급
타로심리상담사 3급

자세한 문의는 010. 7141. 8794
또는 홈페이지를 통해 확인해주세요.

크리스탈힐러심리상담사란 ?

크리스탈 카드를 활용하여 피상담자의 심리상태를 이해하고, 정서적 힐링과 안정을 위한 상담 및 크리스탈카드 상담 프로그램을 교육 및 기획하는 직무를 수행합니다.

자격증 특징

[크리스탈힐러심리상담사] 자격증은 크리스탈과 차크라에 대해 더욱 깊이 배울 수 있으며 프라임뮤즈에서 제작한 [크리스탈 힐링] 카드를 이용할 수 있습니다. 48가지의 원석과, 12가지의 행성카드로 이루어진 [크리스탈 힐링] 카드는 인체상응도와 감각수용도를 포함하고 있어 차크라의 형태, 내담자의 감정/감각에 대한것까지 파악할 수 있습니다.

실제 원석과 겸비하려 보다 높은 수준의 상담을 이어갈 수 있는 매개세로써 적극 활용하시길 바랍니다.

크리스탈힐러심리상담사 자격증 종류

ADVANCED

INTERMEDIATE

BEGINNER

자세한 문의는 010. 7141. 8794

또는 홈페이지를 통해 확인해주세요.

인 사 말

저자 : 고경아

코리아 타로카드, 궁궐비사 편을 구매해주셔서 감사합니다.

이 카드를 제작하면서 너무나 많은 역사적 사실과 방대한 자료 때문에 어떤 것을 넣고 어떤 것을 빼야 할지 많은 고민이 되었습니다.

그중에서도 한국인에게 친숙하지만, 사실은 잘 모르고 있었던 왕족들의 삶과 애환, 그리고 거기에서 평생을 보내야 했던 궁인들의 생활까지도 조금은 가미를 하였고, 아름다운 궁궐의 사계절과 백자 달항아리의 아름다움까지 곁들여서 지루하지 않도록 구성하고자 노력하였습니다.

가장 한국적인 것이 가장 세계적이라는 마음가짐으로 다양한 코리아 디고기드 시리즈를 제작하고 있으니 앞으로 나올 다른 카드들도 많이 애용해주시고 관심을 가져주시기 바랍니다.

처음 이 카드를 접하시는 많은 외국인들께도 한국에 대해서 조금은 알아갈 수 있는 기회가 된다면 더없는 영광이겠습니다. 계속 연구하고 노력해서 다양하고 아름다운 타로카드를 만드는 데 노력하겠습니다.

INTRODUCTION

PRIME MUSE MAIN WRITER. KYOUNGA KO

Thank you for purchasing the Korea Tarot Card – Secret Kingdom.

In the brainstorming stage of the production, it was very difficult for us to decide what stories to include in the cards as we were overwhelmed with the massive amount of historical information.

We eventually chose to depict the joys and sorrows of the royal life as well as the stories of court ladies and palace attendants who were destined to spend their whole lives within the bounds of the palace walls.

Some of these stories are known to Koreans, and yet, not well revealed.

We also tried to make the cards more interesting by kicking in some additional flavors – such as the beautiful four seasons of the palace and elegant white porcelains.

We create the Korea Tarot Card series under the motto that the most Korean is the most global.

We hope that you will stay tuned for our future series.

It is a great honor and privilege for us to be able to introduce the stories of the Korean palace life through our Korea Tarot Card – Secret Kingdom, especially to those who are not familiar with Korean culture.

We will make it a point to bring you a variety of tarot card decks that will introduce you to Korean culture in interesting and beautiful lights.

목 차 한국어

Contents English

宮闕秘史

카 드 설 명

한국어

카드에 대한 간단한 설명과 키워드

1. FORMER KING

궁궐에 앉아서 먼 산을 바라보고 있는 늙은 왕. 예전의 영광을 회상하고 있는 듯하다. 산에는 눈이 내리고 늙은 왕의 머리에도 백발이 앉아있다. 이제는 뒤로 물러앉아서 평화로운 시간을 보내면 되겠지만 아직도 약간의 아쉬움은 남아있다. 과거의 미련을 회상하고 있는 것인지, 아니면 어떤 불미스러운 일들을 후회하고 있는지 알 수 없다. 겉으로 보기에 유유자적한 그의 내면이 어떨지를 알 수 있는 사람은 아무도 없을 것이다. 상왕은 이제 남은 삶을 평화롭게 보내면 될 일이다. 모든 지혜와 경험이 쌓여있지만, 실제 국정운영에는 더 이상 관여하지 않는다. 어떤 왕도 물러날 때를 알아야 하기에 적절한 시기에 물러난 왕에게는 많은 혜택과 영광과 안식이 주어졌다. 천하를 호령하던 호랑이도 나이가 들면 쉴 곳을 찾는 법이다.

Keyword - 지나간 날을 추억함. 현재를 인식해야 할 상황. 퇴직이나 퇴임의 시기. 은퇴 후의 여유로운 시간. 위아래가 분명한 일들. 지휘 체계가 명확한 일에 이로움. 나이 많은 남자의 사연. 왕위의 왕으로서 최고 권력자를 나타내지만 실권은 미미한 상황.

24

2. PAYING RESPECT

안락한 생활을 누리며 안전함이 보장된 상왕의 하루이다. 또한 절대권력자인 왕의 아버지로서의 위엄은 잃지 않았다. 자애로움과 여유가 넘치는 미소에서 그의 편안한 노후를 알아볼 수가 있다. 형식적이지만 결정을 해달라는 두루마리가 책상에 놓여있다. 왕은 아들의 역할을 게을리하지 않기 위해 늘 문안 인사를 여쭙는 것으로 하루 일과를 시작했다. 상왕은 여러 아들 중에서 지금의 왕을 결정하기 위해 많이 고민했을 수도 있다. 조선은 장자가 세자가 되고 왕으로 즉위하는 것이 당연시되었지만 그렇지 못한 경우도 너무나 많았고 왕자의 난이 실제 일어나곤 했다. 그러므로 평화로운 다음 왕이 즉위한다는 것은 상왕으로서의 입장과도 깊이 관계될 수밖에 없었을 것이다. 상왕의 표정이 흐뭇한 깃을 보니 그의 뜻대로 이루어진 듯하다.

Keyword - 아랫사람(권력자. 재력가)으로부터의 문안, 방문, 접촉 모든 것이 거의 다 갖추어진 생활. 그러나 약간의 체제와 관료적인, 정형화된 으레 해야 하는 일에 얽혀있다. 바쁜 가운데에서도 지켜야 할 도리. 형식적인 문서. 높은 사람으로부터의 조언, 나이 많은 남자의 조언.

3. QUEEN DOWAGER

늙었지만 기세등등한 대비의 눈빛에서 모든 것을 쥐고 흔들 수 있다는 야심과 열정을 엿볼 수 있다. 왕실 내에서 의견을 좌우지하는 실세인 듯, 아직도 현역에서 물러나지 않고 조정의 대소사에 관여하고 있는 모습이다. 펼쳐져 있는 책은 보다 진보적인 학문인 듯 보여진다. 백자 항아리에 장식한 꽃은 대비가 품위 있는 취미도 겸하고 있음을 알 수 있다. 궁궐내의 깊은 곳에서 왕을 보좌하며 지내온 지난날의 경험은 백전노장의 것과 다르지 않을 것이다. 후궁들의 견제를 이겨내고 지금의 자리를 지켜오기까지 겪어야 했던 일과 그로 얻어진 지혜를 왕비에게 이야기하고 있는 것 같기도 하다. 왕실의 여인들은 일반 백성들처럼 평범한 시어머니와 며느리의 관계를 떠나서 정치적인 성향과 감각도 중요시하지 않으면 안 되는 운명들이었다.

Keyword – 기품이 있고 나이 많은 여성에게서 도움을 받는다. 평화로운 일상 가운데서도 긴장해야 하는 상황이다. 누군가로부터 허락을 구해야 한다. 안목이 매우 높은 사람과의 만남. 한 가지가 아닌 여러 가지를 모두 잘해 내는 슈퍼 우먼. 노익장 과시. 겉으로 드러난 것이 전부가 아니다.

4. QUEEN MOTHER'S REGENCY

앞에는 쩔쩔매는 어린 왕이 앉아 있고 드리워진 발 뒤에서 근엄한 얼굴의 대비가 버티고 앉아있다. 어린 왕은 그저 꼭두각시에 지나지 않는다. 하지만 이것을 참고 견디면 언젠가는 왕 노릇을 할 희망은 있다. 물론 대비가 물러나 준다는 전제하에 그렇긴 하지만 지금으로선 어쩔 도리가 없다. 실속 없는 어린 권력자는 한동안은 진정한 힘을 휘두르지 못하는 상황일 것이다. 대비는 자신의 사람으로 주변을 배치하고 어린 왕이 영원히 판단력 없는 군주가 되길 바라는지도 모른다. 조선의 왕들 중에는 수명이 길지 않아서 자기 아들이 충분히 통치할만한 나이가 되기 전에 세상을 떠나게 되어 대비가 수렴청정하게 되는 경우가 종종 있었다.

Keyword – 허수아비 노릇을 어느 기긴 동안은 할 수밖에 없다. 참고 인내하는 시기. 다른 사람들은 모르는 고통의 시간이다. 겉으로는 화려하지만, 실속 없는 상태. 앞에 보이는 것이 전부가 아니다. 뒤에 또 다른 조종자가 있다. 두 명의 윗사람을 모셔야 하는 상황. 진퇴양난. 지나친 간섭으로 성숙하기 힘들다.

5. ROYAL AUDIENCE

드디어 왕은 자신이 원하는 옥좌에 앉았다. 앞에는 신하들이 조아리고 있고, 먼 곳을 응시하는 왕은 자신의 영광스러운 미래를 내다보는 듯하다. 뒤에는 왕권을 상징하는 일월오악도가 그려져 있다. 특히 이 그림은 아시아에서도 조선 왕실에만 그려진 그림으로서 특히 왕의 집무 공간에서 전 우주를 통찰하며 자연과 조화된 왕이 신격화 되는 비유로서 배치되었다. 사실 왕의 하루 일정은 매우 복잡하고 다단했으며 정무를 돌보는 데도 많은 시간이 할애되었지만, 왕실 가족의 대소사를 살펴보고 사신 접견은 물론 신하들의 출신과 성향에 따라 갈라진 의견을 하나로 조율하는 것에 늘 신경을 곤두세우지 않으면 안 되었다. 왕의 아래에 머리를 조아리고 있는 신하들 중에는 내심 자신들의 이익을 어떻게 더 요구할 수 있을지가 관심사일 수도 있었다.

Keyword – 이보다 더 행복할 수 없는 시간. 능력과 지성과 젊음을 두루 갖춘 완전체, 여러 사람들의 공경을 받음, 가장 높은 지위에 올라감. 일반 사람들과 견줄 수 없는 위대함, 탁월함, 만인의 위에 군림하는 자. 존경과 권위를 가지고 있는 사람을 만나다. 이해관계가 다르지만 매우 가까이 있는 자들.

28

6. QUEEN TAKING A STROLL

한껏 치장하고 정원을 거니는 왕비의 모습이다. 왕비는 모처럼의 한가한 시간을 내어서 정원에서 무성하게 물든 단풍나무 아래에 서서 그 빛깔에 탐복하며 나무를 만져보고 있다. 모든 것이 원숙하게 되어 무르익은 모습이다. 왕비는 자신의 인생에서 가장 빛나는 시기를 보내고 있으며 정원의 나무 또한 일 년 중에 가장 아름답게 자신을 뽐내고 있다. 내명부라고 해서 궁궐의 안주인인 왕비는 후궁과 모든 여인들과 관련된 것을 정비하고 지시하고 다스리는 책임과 의무가 있었다. 그렇기에 자신의 취향을 드러내기보다는 왕실에 큰 잡음이 일어나지 않도록 하고 왕이 정무에 힘쓸 수 있도록 돕는 것이 가장 큰 덕목이었다. 또한 왕자를 낳은 왕비는 그 자리가 더욱 탄탄해져서 그야말로 여인으로서는 최고의 영예를 누리게 되었다.

Keyword - 성숙한 단계에 올라서다. 배경과 주인공이 하나가 됨. 여건이 넉넉하고 모든 것이 어우러진다. 망중한의 여유로움이 보기 좋다. 잠시나마 외부로 나가서 자신의 여유를 즐긴다. 짧지만 좋은 휴식. 스스로도 최고의 상태이며 주변 여건도 매우 만족스럽다.

7. ROYAL WEDDING

왕과 왕비의 결혼식은 화려함의 절정이다. 역시 뒤
에는 왕권을 상징하는 일월오악도가 그려져 있고 왕
과 왕비를 상징하는 해와 달이 오늘만큼은 실제 주인
공들로 대체 되었다. 백성들을 향해서 두 사람이 혼
인하였음을 널리 알리고 천지에 이를 고하며 새로운
시대를 열어가는 날이다. 왕은 정략적인 결혼이 매우
당연하였으며 당대에 가장 어울리는 존귀한 집안의
여성을 맞이하여 혼인하였다. 물론 그 전에 여러 명
의 신부 후보들을 두고 누구를 맞이하는가 하는 문제
도 본인의 의지는 거의 반영되지 않았다. 왕은 세자
의 신분일 때에 결혼하기도 했고 왕위에 즉위한 후에
결혼식을 치르는 경우도 있었다. 모든 것을 쥔 한 나
라의 군주라고 하더라도 아내를 맞이하는 일에 본인
의 의견이 그다지 크게 작용하지 않는다는 점은 참으
로 아이러니한 일이다.

Keyword - 의견의 합일, 성취, 일이 성사됨. 큰 계
약일수록 더욱 유리하게 성사되고 작은 일에는 만족
감이 덜 할 수도 있다. 사랑하는 사람들은 결실을 보
게 되며 새로운 전환점이 생긴다. 위대한 결합. 동업
에 성사됨이 길하고 등을 돌렸던 문제들도 긍정적인
방향으로 급전환 된다.

8. COURT LADIES

나름대로 꾸미고 치장한 궁녀들 세 명 정도가 방에 앉아서 노리개와 비녀 등을 가지고 자랑하고 있다. 자기들이 모시는 윗전의 험담을 하기도 하고 소문을 주고받고 있다. 악의는 없지만, 이들에게서 흘러나가는 이야기는 나중에 큰 소란을 가져올 수가 있다. 사람이 많은 곳에는 말도 많고 탈도 많다. 낮말은 새가 듣고 밤말은 쥐가 듣는다는 속담이 제격인 장면이다. 이들이 손에 들고 자랑하는 노리개나 비녀는 자신들의 월급으로는 살 수 없는 고가의 귀중품들이다. 분명히 자신들의 윗전에서 선물로 받은 것이든지 다른 경로를 통해서 입수한 것일 것이다. 이들은 사는 형편이 어려워서 입궁한 경우가 많았기에 이러한 물건으로도 쉽게 매수되곤 했었다. 저 멀리서 이들의 대화를 엿듣는 그림자가 이러한 어두운 비태를 암시하는 것만 같다.

Keyword - 철부지들의 행동. 소시민의 즐거움. 작은 험담이 불러오는 큰 불행. 입조심을 해야 한다. 낮말은 새가 듣고 밤말은 쥐가 듣는다. 사람들이 어울리는 곳에 가게 되면 말도 많고 탈도 많다. 도토리 키재기. 수준이 비슷한 사람들과의 어울림

9. ARCHERY BY CROWN PRINCE

왕과 왕비의 아들이며 세자로 책봉이 된 듯하다. 그러나 궁궐 뒤뜰에서 몰래 활쏘기 연습을 하고 있는 표정에서 화풀이하는 것처럼 보이기도 한다. 옆의 내시는 눈치를 보기 바쁘고 나뭇가지에 앉은 새 한 마리가 화살 소리에 놀라 소란스럽게 날개를 퍼덕인다. 그래도 과녁을 맞춘 화살이 많은 것으로 보아 자신의 소신대로 밀고 나가려는 듯한 성격을 엿볼 수 있다. 조선의 왕들이 정치를 잘하기 위해서는 무력과 싸움에 능하기보다는 지식과 덕망이 우선시 되어야 했는데 세자의 이러한 과격한 성향은 왕의 마음에 그다지 들지 않을 수도 있다고 짐작해본다. 태조 이성계가 혁명으로 고려왕조를 끝내고 조선왕조를 새로이 연 것은 맞지만 이후에는 문관 성향의 왕들이 집권하기를 원했고 그러한 것이 전통이 되었기 때문이다.

Keyword - 작은 야망. 남몰래 미래를 계획하고 있지만, 아직 겉으로 드러내기에는 시기상조. 혼자만의 시간을 견디어야 한다. 남에게 내보일 수 없는 처지. 주변에 그다지 돕는 인연이 나타나지 않는다. 큰 위험은 아니지만 고립된 상황이다. 좋은 자리에 있음에도 누리지를 못한다.

10. EMBROIDERY BY PRINCESS

어린 공주가 수를 놓고 있다. 창문이 닫힌 채로 앉아서 나름대로 집중하는 모습이 매우 진지하다. 밖에 나가서 한참 뛰어놀고 싶은 나이일 텐데 자신의 지위에 걸맞은 생활을 하고자 노력하고 있는 모습이 성숙해 보인다. 왕족으로 태어났다는 것은 매우 행운이지만 그 위치를 지키고자 어릴 때부터 갖추어야 할 소양 교육은 매우 엄격했다. 특히 공주들은 태어나면서부터 앞으로 자신들이 살아가야 할 운명이 정해져 있었다. 왕가에서 정해주는 귀한 가문의 자제들과 혼인을 해서 살아가야 했고 대부분 공주를 며느리로 맞이하는 집안에서는 웃어른을 모시고 사는 것과 같은 분위기여서 딱히 반가운 혼처라고 보기는 어려웠다. 하지만 집안의 지위 상승을 위해서는 매우 좋은 기회가 되기도 했다.

Keyword – 조숙함. 차분하게 일을 진행할 수 있다. 어리지만 고귀한 여성. 배우고 익혀야 할 시기. 지위에 맞는 생활을 하기 위해선 포기해야 할 것들이 있다. 일반적이지 않은 삶과 생활. 출생이나 근본이 매우 훌륭하며 그에 어울리는 인격과 기술 또한 함께 갖추어짐.

33

11. PRINCE PLAYING TAG

궁인들과 함께 단풍이 흐드러진 마당에서 장난을 치고 있는 왕자. 그러나 위험하게도 발 앞에 돌부리가 있음을 보지 못한 채 금방이라도 걸려서 넘어질 것 같은 상황이다. 물론 잘 비켜 갈 수도 있을 것이다. 그러나 발이라도 걸리면 존엄한 왕자는 상처를 입게 될 것이다. 그러면 같이 놀아주던 궁인들이 큰 벌을 받을 것은 당연지사여서 늘 조마조마하게 주변 사람들은 긴장해야 했다. 아무리 나이가 어리더라도 함부로 대할 수 없는 존귀한 존재였기 때문이다. 왕자 형제들이 많으면 그들의 미래는 단 한 명의 세자를 제외하고는 모두 알 수 없는 운명으로 살아가야 했는데, 왕에게 누가 되지 않기 위해 서기도 했고 왕좌를 넘보는 이가 있다면 거기에 이용되는 불행도 겪어야 했기 때문이다. 아직 자신의 운명이 어떻게 될지는 정해지지 않은 걸 아는지 모르는지 천진난만하게 웃는 왕자의 얼굴에는 근심이 없다.

Keyword - 모든 것을 다 갖춘 사람에게도 찾아오는 위기. 안전해 보이는 것 가운데 위험이 도사리고 있다. 그저 스쳐 지나갈 위험일 수도 있다. 다른 사람 옆에서 괜히 거들다가 큰 낭패를 볼 수도 있다. 생각없이 기분 따라 한 행동에 책임을 져야 할 수도 있다. 미숙한 행동으로 인한 실수.

34

12. SPY

먼동이 터오는 어스름한 새벽에 매의 발에 매어놓은 편지를 받는 첩자의 얼굴이 의미심장하다. 궁궐 밖의 사람과 무슨 내용을 주고받는 것인지는 알 수 없지만 남의 눈을 피해서 몰래 연락을 주고받는다는 점에서 왕을 위한 것이 아니라는 것만은 확실히 알 수 있다. 궁궐은 넓고 많은 이들이 상주하고 있었기에 일일이 이들의 충성심을 확인할 방법은 없었다. 또한 그들이 벌이는 일들을 완전무결하게 감시할 방법도 없었다. 어떨 때는 감시를 해야 하는 책무를 맡은 자가 첩자 노릇을 하는 경우도 있었다. 이들은 자신의 신념에 따른 행동을 하기도 했지만, 자기들이 따르는 윗전의 하수인인 경우가 더 많았다. 그 보상으로는 당연히 많은 재물과 신분 상승의 기회가 약속되었을 것이다. 그러나 영원한 비밀은 없기에 그들이 벌이는 일들이 성공할지는 미지수이다.

Keyword - 가까운 곳에 배신자가 있다. 남의 눈에 띄지 않게 진행되는 일. 시기상조. 아직 겉으로 드러나지 않은 계획들. 나보다 신분이 낮은 사람들 중에 의혹을 살만한 인물이 있다. 좀처럼 밝혀내기 어려운 일. 계략, 농간. 기다리던 소식이 도착한다. 상대방이나 나에게 어느 쪽이 유리한지 지금은 알 수 없다

13. BIRTH OF PRINCE

막 태어난 왕자가 비단 강보에 싸여있다. 상왕과 왕이 같이 기뻐하며 왕조의 앞날이 탄탄해짐에 감격하고 있다. 창문 너머로 아침의 찬란한 태양이 떠오르며 미래의 위대한 군주가 될 암시를 보여준다. 나라의 가장 위대한 권력자 둘의 사랑을 한 몸에 받는 왕자에게는 모든 것이 약속되어있다. 이렇듯 태어나면서 왕좌가 보장되기도 했지만, 역사의 소용돌이 속에서 당연한 자신의 자리를 차지하지도 못한 채 밀려나는 불운한 왕도 매우 많았다. 왕실에서는 왕자가 태어나지 않으면 매우 불안해했는데 현대와 달리 혈통으로 대대손손 이어져야만 했기 때문이다. 만일 세자가 될 왕자가 태어나지 않는다면 왕의 갑작스러운 사망 후에 서로 옹립하는 왕자들을 내세운 무리들이 첨예한 쟁탈전을 벌일 것은 불을 보듯 훤한 일이었다.

Keyword - 지금 이제 무언가 일이 시작되었다. 위대한 첫걸음. 보장된 입지에서 시작하는 여정. 본격적이지 않더라도 미리 계획된 운명의 수레바퀴. 자신의 뜻과는 전혀 상관이 없는 큰 흐름. 숙명적으로 얽힌 인연. 남들에게 모두 소문이 날 만한 좋은 일이나 축하받을 만한 경사.

14. SHAMAN'S RITUAL

왕족에 의해서 궁궐로 몰래 들어온 무당이 어떤 의
식을 행하고 있다. 앞에 앉은 왕실의 여인들은 무슨
소원을 빌고 있는지 자못 심각하고 진지하다. 신이 실
려서 눈에 살기가 등등한 무당이 뭔가 공수를 내리고
있는 중이다. 하지만 이는 정식적으로 허가된 행사
가 아니라 비밀스럽게 진행되는 의식이어서 들키게
되면 추궁을 당하거나 처벌을 받을 수도 있었다. 왕
비나 후궁들을 비롯한 왕실의 여인들은 아들을 낳게
해달라거나 왕의 사랑을 더 받을 수 있게 해달라거나
하는 것이 주된 소원이었는데 만일 누군가의 한이 서
려 있다든가 좋지 않은 기운이 있어서 방해된다면 그
것을 해소해줄 사람으로 무당을 청하기도 했다. 여인
들만 기거하는 깊은 궁궐이어서 궁인들의 입만 단속
한다면 왕의 귀에 들어가지 않고 종종 이러한 의식을
행할 수 있었다.

Keyword - 비공식적인 루트를 통해서 일을 처리
하려고 함. 마음에 쌓인 것을 해소하게 됨. 자신의 힘
으로 되지 않으니 초자연적인 것에 의존하려고 함.
들키게 되면 떳떳하지 못한 행위. 원한 관계로 빚어
진 일일 수도 있다. 마음속에 오랫동안 염원하던 일
을 해결함.

15. ROYAL PLACENTA CHAMBER

일반 백성들에게도 아기가 태어나면 탯줄을 잘 보관하는 풍습이 있었는데 왕실에서는 더할 나위가 없었다. 탯줄에 왠지 모를 힘과 효험이 있으리란 막연한 믿음 때문이었다. 아기가 태어났을 때 그 부산물인 탯줄을 소중히 여기는 풍습은 꽤 오래된 역사를 갖고 있다. 일반인은 아이가 태어나면 그 탯줄을 소중히 보관했다가 불로 태우거나 물에 띄워 보내면서 다음 아이의 잉태에 재앙이 없기를 기원한다. 미래에 존귀한 왕이 될 왕자가 태어나면 그의 태를 묻은 장소를 잘 선정하여 이렇게 장엄하게 장식하고 관리를 하며 매우 신성하게 여겼다. 태실을 알리는 석물 위에 나비가 한 마리 앉아있다. 조상의 영혼을 나비로 생각한다면 왕실의 선조들이 왕자가 태어남을 축하한다는 의미로 여겨도 좋을 것이다. 주변은 바야흐로 꽃이 만발하여 음산한 무덤이 아닌 왕자의 아름다운 미래를 기약하고 있다.

Keyword - 이제 영광된 일이 일어나려고 있다. 위대한 시작의 첫걸음. 비밀스러운 자들의 모임이나 약속, 기념비적인 사건. 또는 증거물. 큰 조직하에서 움직이는 일들이며 정해진 순서대로 차례차례 진행된다. 감히 나서서 훼손하거나 망칠 수 없을 만큼 관료적인 행사.

16. KING'S HUNTING

말을 타고 사냥 중인 젊은 왕의 모습에서 활력이
느껴진다. 왕은 종종 신하들에게 그 위용을 보이기 위
해서 사냥을 일부러 주도하기도 했다. 물론 전란 시에
직접 전투에 나서는 경우도 있었지만 매우 드물었고
평소에는 지위가 높은 무관들과 어울리면서 왕의 권
력을 각인시키는 시간을 가졌던 것으로 보인다. 그러
나 그것도 왕의 취향에 어느 정도는 맞아야 이루어지
는 행사였다. 강력한 중앙집권체제를 이룩하기 위해
귀족들이 사병을 갖는 것을 금하던 시절이어서 모든
병사는 왕의 것이었다. 저 멀리 뒤따르는 무장들과 신
분이 높은 사람들도 보인다. 그런데 불행하게도 큰 곰
이 나무 뒤에 그늘에 숨어서 지나가는 무리를 노리고
있다. 어느 누가 희생될지 알 수 없고, 오히려 곰이 희
생될 수도 있을 것이다. 일촉즉발의 상황이지만 왕은
사냥에 열중해서 전혀 모르고 있다.

Keyword – 큰 이동수가 있다. 움직여야지 소득이
있다. 그러나 뜻하지 않은 위험도 있으니 조심할 것.
호응하는 사람들이 있지만 결국에는 나 혼자 감당해
야 하는 일이 될 수도 있다. 먼 거리 여행이나 출장에
서 얻게 되는 이익이 기대되지만 조심할 것은 조심
해야 한다. 허망하게 수포로 돌아갈 수 있으니 조심.

17. PROCESSION TO TEMPORARY PALACE

거대한 행렬이며 왕이 직접 다른 궁궐로 행차를 하는 모습이다. 신하들과 나팔수의 장엄한 행렬이 함께하며 왕권의 위대함을 백성들에게 보여준다. 이는 임시로 궁궐을 나와서 다른 궁궐로 이동하는 행차인데 백성들의 삶을 살펴보고 지방 순시를 하는 정치적인 목적 이외에도 왕권 강화를 위한 다른 목적 또한 충분히 달성하였다. 현명한 왕은 자신의 궁궐에만 머물러 있지 않고 이렇게 정기적으로 큰 인원과 자금을 동원하여 백성들에게 볼거리를 제공하여 자신의 치세를 만천하에 알리는 데 힘썼다. 그것은 현대의 기준으로 본다고 해도 대단한 정치적 감각이 아닐 수 없었다.

Keyword – 이사를 하든지 생활의 기초를 모두 바꾸는 큰 이동이 있다. 원거리 이동, 해외로 이동, 유학. 여러 사람이 함께 이동하는 대규모의 활동에 더욱 적합할 수도 있다. 한꺼번에 두 마리의 토끼를 잡을 수 있다. 겉으로 보이는 목적과 속에 감춘 진짜 목적이 따로 있다.

18. SIXTIETH BIRTHDAY

궁궐의 맨 웃어른으로서 매우 영예로운 순간이다. 왕실 사람이라고 해서 수명이 긴 것만은 아니었기 때문에 회갑연 등을 맞이한다는 건 큰 의미가 있었다. 대비에게도 젊은 시절이 분명히 있었으며 어린 나이에 궁궐에 들어와 말할 수 없는 세월을 보내야 했을 것이다. 늘 즐겁고 화려한 시절만 있었던 것도 아니며 아무에게도 이야기하지 못한 채 자신의 마음속에 묻어야만 했던 회한에 찬 날도 많았을지 모른다. 괴로운 시기가 지난 뒤에 그에 맞는 보답이 온다는 것을 알려주는 듯 대비는 감회에 찬 상기된 표정이다. 한편으로는 자신이 지금까지 이룩해놓은 것에 대한 자부심일 수도 있으리라. 남편인 왕은 정치를 했지만 결국 자신의 아들이 다시 왕이 될 것은 자명한 사실이기 때문이다.

Keyword – 큰 행사를 앞두고 있음. 매우 화려한 연회. 격조 있는 모임에 초대되거나 그것을 준비해야 할 수도 있다. 내가 만일 모임의 주인공이라면 마냥 기뻐할 수는 없고 그에 걸맞은 자격을 유지해야 하는 숙제가 존재한다. 어쨌거나 경사로운 날이다. 남들로부터 주목을 받는다.

19. PLEAS TO KING

골치가 아픈 왕의 모습과는 달리 간신배로 보이는 신하는 절을 하며 꿍꿍이가 있는 미소를 짓고 있다. 어쩌면 왕을 애먹이기 위해서 미리 준비한 상소를 올린 것일 수도 있다. 그것을 모르는 왕은 매우 난처한 상황에 처한다. 왕을 위해 일을 해야 하는 신하이지만 그는 정작 자신의 이득을 위해 왕을 이용하는 것일 수도 있다. 왕은 자신과 입장을 같이 하는 무리와 아닌 무리를 잘 구별해야만 했다. 조선은 당파 싸움이 그치질 않았는데 이 문제는 늘 해결하기 어려운 고질병과도 같았다. 파벌싸움을 그만두고 백성을 위해 그 힘을 하나로 모아야 하는 것은 지금도 다르지 않다. 왕과 신하의 팽팽한 대결이다.

Keyword – 서로 입장이 다름. 표리부동한 자들을 곁에 두고 있음을 유의하라. 하극상이 이루어질 수도 있다. 나에게 문제 거리를 가져다주는 사람과 만나야만 한다. 가장 가까이 있는 사람을 조심해야 한다. 겉으로 보이는 것이 전부는 아니다. 결국은 나에게 손해가 될 사람이 옆에 있다.

20. ASKING FOR FORGIVENESS

왕족이 잘못했을 때 의관을 벗고 바닥에 앉아서 죄를 사하여 주시기를 왕에게 바라는 의식이다. 왕의 용서가 있을 때까지 이 의식은 밤이고 낮이고 계속된다. 어떨 때는 기력을 잃고 쓰러지기도 했다. 화려한 의관을 모두 벗고 평민으로 돌아와서 죄를 구하는 이러한 때는 중죄보다도 왕의 심사를 거스르는 경우가 많았다. 왕가의 법도는 일반 백성들과 다른 점이 있었는데 그중에서도 아버지와 아들의 관계에서 특히 그러했다. 왕과 다음의 왕이 될 세자의 관계는 군신의 관계도 같이 겸했기에 불효가 아닌 불충에 대하여서도 그 여부가 판단되곤 했다. 아무리 효심에서 우러나오는 언행이라고 하더라도 그것이 현재의 왕에게 불충한 것이라면 죄가 될 수도 있었다. 물론 주변의 부추김 또한 없지 않았다.

Keyword - 많은 여유가 있음에도 위기가 닥침. 관재구설이 발생하니 매우 조심해야 할 때. 섣부른 행동으로 화를 덧붙여서는 안 될 것이다. 내 잘못이 아닌 남의 잘못을 대신해서 짊어져야 할지도 모른다. 자존심을 모두 내려놓을 일이 생긴다. 평소 대처하지 않아서 큰 화를 부른다.

21. DANCERS

달이 뜬 밤에 누각에 주연상이 벌어졌다. 왕과 핵심 신하들이 간만의 여유를 즐기며 담소를 나누고 있고 무희들이 춤을 추고 있다. 그러나 앞의 여인은 왠지 다른 생각에 잠겨있는 표정이다. 춤을 추다가 갑자기 품 안의 칼을 뽑고 달려들지도 모를 일이다. 아니면 자신의 연인을 생각하고 있는지도 모른다. 이처럼 같은 주연 자리에서도 저마다 각각의 입장은 천차만별이 아닐 수 없다. 왕궁의 주연을 준비하기 위해서 전문 무용수들은 늘 준비하고 연습을 게을리하지 않았는데 때로는 외국에서 들어온 예술단과도 같이 공연을 선보이곤 했다. 궁궐 안에 있긴 해도 고급문화와 유흥에 있어서는 그 소문이 담장을 넘어 밖에서 흘러들어왔으며 이에 이것을 즐기긴 해도 지나치다는 평을 듣지 않기 위해 조절을 해야만 했다.

Keyword – 자칫 잘못하면 방탕하게 될 수도 있지만, 때에 따라서는 필요한 향락의 과정. 잘 활용하면 도움이 될 수도 있다. 서로 입장이 분명히 다른 사람들이 모여있다. 내가 주인공이 아닌 상황을 직시해야 한다. 화려하게 보이지만 실속 없이 남의 잔치에 초대된 것일 수도 있다.

44

22. KING'S MORNING ASSEMBLY

왕이 아침 조회에 근엄한 표정으로 앉아 있고 대신들이 머리를 조아리고 있다. 평소와는 다르게 무관들이 앞에 지키고 있는 것으로 봐서 신하들의 의지를 꺾고 왕의 고집대로 정책을 통과시키려 하든가 아니면 간신배를 처단하기 위한 것으로 보인다. 진정한 왕권이 무엇인가를 보여주려 하는 장면인 듯하다. 아니면 마침내 신하들 중의 몇몇은 죄상이 낱낱이 밝혀질 참인지도 모른다. 늘 이들에게 좌우지되던 왕이 아닌 것이다. 왕은 오랜 기간 숙고한 끝에 드디어 자신만의 정치를 펼치기 위해서 큰 결단을 내렸다. 이렇게 하지 않으면 하라는 대로 하는 허수아비 왕에 지나지 않을 것이기 때문이다.

Keyword - 빠른 시일 내에 결과를 알게 된다. 공식적 문서가 하달된다. 사적인 부분에서는 불리하다. 결정의 순간이 왔기에 더는 미룰 수가 없다. 판단해야만 하는 상황이 된다. 아니면 내가 남의 판단을 받아야 하는 상황이 되거나 공식적인 절차에 들어가게 된다.

45

23. ROYAL ANCESTRAL SHRINE

역대 왕과 왕비의 신위를 봉안한 사당이다. 동아시아의 유교적 왕실 제례 건축으로서 공간계획 방식이 매우 독특하고 우수하다. 세계적인 건축가들의 경탄을 받아온 건물로 단순하지만, 압도적인 분위기는 왕조의 혼령들을 모신 장엄함을 연출한다. 왕조의 정통성과 권력에 당위성을 부여하며 왕조 자체를 상징하는 기능을 잘 수행하고 있다. 왕들은 어릴 때부터 이곳을 드나들며 자신들의 혈통과 전통이 어디에서 유래되는지를 배웠고 마음속에 새겨야만 했다. 그러므로 자신의 운명이 어떻게 나아가야 할 것인가를 스스로 깨우쳐 갔던 것이다. 어떤 왕이 되어야 할지는 여기에 모셔진 위대한 왕들의 업적과 생애에서 충분히 배울 수 있었으며 먼 후일 자신 또한 여기에 안치될 것을 생각하며 자신의 한걸음이 얼마나 무거운 가를 느끼고 감당해야 했을 것이다.

Keyword - 추상적인 부분에 매우 강력하며 현실성이 떨어지는 일면이 있다. 힘든 오늘을 살아가야 할 평범한 사람들에겐 불리한 카드이지만 권력자나 지위가 있는 사람에게는 좋은 카드가 될 수도 있다. 사람의 머릿속을 지배하고 있는 가장 중심 개념. 지나간 날의 부귀영화.

24. DEATH OF KING

고복의식이라고 해서 우리 민족의 전통적인 상례
의식이기도 하다. 고복이란 임종한 사람을 그립고 안
타까워하는 마음으로 돌아와 달라며 곡을 하는 것을
말하는데, 이 일은 왕을 가까이서 모시던 내시가 주로
맡아서 한다. 상선이나 그 아래 내시가 왕족의 시신이
입고 있던 옷을 벗겨내 죽음을 맞이한 궁의 지붕으로
올라가 북쪽을 향해 '상위복' 이라고 세 번을 외치는
데 죽음의 길로 가지 말고 돌아오라는 뜻으로 대비나
중전은 "중궁복"이라고 외쳤다. 지붕에 있던 내시가
고복을 하고 옷을 던지면 지붕 아래에 있던 또 다른
내시가 옷을 받아서 함에 넣어간 다음 임종한 왕족의
시신을 덮어주고 곡을 시작하며 이 의식이 끝나면 곧
바로 국상을 선포하게 된다. 새로운 왕이 등극하는 새
로운 시대가 열리는 것이다.

Keyword – 슬픔이 있지만 하나의 시대가 지나가
고 새로운 것이 도달함. 지나간 것에 미련을 두지 않
는 것이 좋다. 온 곳으로 돌아감. 운명의 시간이 다가
옴. 작별하는 것에는 의미가 있다. 모든 위대한 것의
최후. 큰일이 대단원의 막을 내린다.

47

25. PLAY BLINDFOLD TAG

아름다운 꽃들이 만발한 봄날에 뜰에서 어린 공주가 눈을 가린 채 궁인들과 술래잡기를 하고 있다. 사실 꽃보다 더 아름다운 것은 공주의 젊은 날일 것이다. 아직 혼례를 올리지 않았기도 했지만, 왕자의 의무가 없기에 조금은 가벼운 마음으로 자신의 삶을 향유할 수 있는 여유 있는 모습이기도 하다. 공주는 미래의 생활이 보장된 삶을 살았고 웬만해서는 왕족의 지위를 박탈당하지 않았다. 그만큼 조선 시대에는 여인들의 활동이나 사회진출은 소극적이었고 궁궐 내에서도 그다지 많은 활동무대가 주어지지 않았다.

Keyword – 아직은 서투른 시작이지만 거의 모든 것이 갖추어져 있는 풍족한 생활. 인생의 봄날.가족이나 가문의 배경이 든든한 사람. 고귀한 신분이며 보장된 미래. 지금은 자신에게 주어진 행복한 나날을 충분히 누려도 되는 시절. 높은 신분의 여자. 나이가 어린 여자.

26. STATE EXAMINATION

많은 선비들이 과거 시험을 보고 있다. 저마다 장원급제의 꿈을 안고 있기도 하고 합격하여 작은 관리라도 되기를 희망한다. 글을 써내려가는 사람들의 표정이 매우 진지하다. 이렇게 해서 집안을 일으키고 가문의 영광이 되는 기회가 되고자 저마다 선의의 경쟁을 기울이고 있다. 전혀 예상하지 못한 주제가 주어진다면 그 답을 적고자 모든 역량을 발휘해야 할 것이다. 그 시절에도 몇 년에 걸쳐서 낙방하여 관리의 길에 나아가지 못하는 사례가 수두룩하였으나 일찍이 소년등과하여 천재성을 인정받아 20대 초반의 나이에 벌써 중요한 관직에 앉는 경우도 심심치 않게 있어왔다.

Keyword - 시험을 본 일이 있다. 문서운과 관련이 있다. 오랫동안 준비한 일이 본격적으로 진행됨. 아직 결과가 나오지는 않지만, 그 과정이 매우 중요하다. 집중하지 않으면 안 되는 일. 이번 기회에 판가름이 나는 일. 꼭 풀어야만 하는 숙제를 안게 된다. 테스트 앞두고 있다. 만반의 준비.

49

27. PRISONER

목에 칼을 차고 머리가 산발이 된 사람이 감옥 안에 갇혀 있다. 그 앞에는 엎질러버린 밥그릇이 보인다. 자신은 죄가 없기 때문에 이러한 대접이 마땅치 않다는 표현이기도 하다. 표정 또한 아직 꺾이지 않은 자신의 의지를 관철하고자 하는 눈빛이 강렬하다. 이 모든 사연을 다 아는 듯한 포졸이 오히려 눈치를 보고 있다. 원래는 죄인이 매우 지체 높은 사람이었을 수도 있다. 죄가 없음에도 파벌싸움에 연루되어 억울하게 옥살이를 하고 귀양을 가는 것도 허다한 시절이었다. 심하게는 죽음을 맞이하기도 했는데 뒤늦게 오명이 벗겨져 사후에 다시 그 명예가 회복되기도 하였다.

Keyword - 힘들지만 예상치 못한 반전 미래가 기다리고 있다. 자신의 뜻을 굽히지 않는 사람과의 만남. 또는 나의 뜻이 관철되지 않는 답답한 상황. 어려움 속에서도 자존심을 잃으면 안 된다. 누명을 쓸 일이 생긴다. 당분간은 자신의 입장이 밝혀지기 어려운 시간이다.

28. LAZY CROWN PRINCE

　대학자들을 스승으로 둔 세자는 대낮의 수업이 지겹기 짝이 없다. 게다가 식곤증이 온 건지 장난기가 발동한 것인지 책에다 낙서까지 하다가 침을 흘리며 졸기 시작한다. 자신들의 역할을 완수해야 하는 학자들은 난감하기 이를 데가 없다. 이를 방관해도 벌을 받을 것이요 말 안 듣는 세자를 가르치자니 하루가 너무나 길게 느껴질 뿐이다. 학문에 뜻이 없고 바깥 활동을 즐기는 체질인 탓에 성군이 되기 위해 읽어야 하는 많은 책은 고문일 수도 있었다. 물론 나라의 군주가 되는 것에 있어서 이론이 전부는 아니었다. 하지만 배울 만큼 배운 대신들을 호령하기 위해서는 게을리할 수 없는 공부이기도 했다.

　Keyword - 어리지만 함부로 대할 수 없는 사람과의 만남. 당분간은 이 관계를 지속해야 한다. 입장이 다른 사람들과의 생활. 울지도 웃지도 못하는 상황. 심각한 사건이라고 보기는 어렵지만 나태한 습관으로 인해서 결국은 좋지 않은 결과가 생겨날 것이다. 철부지의 휴식.

51

29. COURT LADIES PAID SALARIES

급여를 받고 기뻐하는 궁녀들이 줄을 지어서 자신
의 차례를 기다리고 있다. 궁인들은 정해진 날에 자
신들의 급여를 챙겨서 받았다. 왕에 대한 충성도 있지
만, 실제 자신들의 자유와 바꾼 대가로서 생활이 풍족
해지는 것에 대한 만족감을 볼 수가 있다. 이 돈으로
는 밖에 있는 자신들의 가족의 궁핍한 살림살이에 보
태는 경우도 있었다. 또 궁녀로 늙어서 퇴직하여 궁
을 나간다든가 할 경우에 자신의 노후를 위해서 차곡
차곡 모으기도 했다. 극심한 가뭄이 온다거나 흉년이
지면 궁녀들을 대거 궁 밖으로 내보내어 비가 내리기
를 바라는 의식도 거행했지만, 그전에는 딱히 궁을 나
가고 싶다고 해서 나갈 수 있는 것이 아니었기에 자신
의 노후준비는 알아서 해야만 했다.

Keyword – 매우 현실적인 행복. 작은 것에서 보람
된 것을 찾는 게 좋다. 거창한 것보다는 소소한 것에
서 이득을 본다. 자신만의 영역에서 발견되는 기쁨.
남과는 다른 것을 발견한다. 생활 속의 소망이 이루
어진다. 큰 목적보다는 눈앞의 현실적인 작은 목적이
더 빨리 이루어진다.

30. PRINCE AND PAUPER

민담에서 내려오는 이야기일 수 있지만, 실제 일어
났던 사건을 기반으로 하는 것일 수도 있다. 얼굴이
같은 왕자와 거지는 우연히 만나서 장난삼아 서로의
옷을 바꿔 입게 된다. 이로 인하여 결론이 어떻게 날
지는 전혀 알 수 없는 상황이다. 왕자가 영원히 자신
의 자리로 돌아오지 못하게 될지, 혹은 나중에 탄로
가 나서 거지는 경을 치게 될 수도 있다. 화려하고 모
든 것이 다 갖추어졌음에도 갑갑한 궁궐의 생활이 싫
었던 왕자나 비참한 처지에서 벗어날 수 없었던 거지
나 둘 다 모두 자신의 운명을 잠시라도 바꿀 수만 있
다면 어떻게든 한 번만이라도 해보고 싶었던 소박한
바람일 수도 있겠다.

Keyword - 서로 입장이 뒤바뀌게 됨, 예상치 못
한 변동, 미래를 알 수 없는 사람들과 어울리게 됨. 매
우 밀착된 관계지만 매우 위험한 도박이다. 치기 어
린 행동. 심사숙고하지 않은 행위에 대해서는 책임을
져야만 할 것이다. 자신의 기분을 내기 위해서 어리
석은 선택을 한다.

31. PALACE PHARMACY

약을 짓고 있는 궁내의 의원과 의녀. 의젓하게 약을 만들고 있는 의녀를 흐뭇하게 바라보는 나이 든 의원에게서 관록이 느껴진다. 매달린 약봉지와 약재들은 이들의 것이 아니라 왕족을 위한 것이다. 전문적인 분야이기도 하고 왕족의 건강을 책임지고 있는 곳이기 때문에 매우 엄격하게 관리되었다. 약간의 착오라도 있어서는 목이 달아날 수 있는 곳이었다. 따라서 당대에 가장 실력 있는 의사와 약사들이 모두 이곳에 근무하고 있었다. 이들조차 해결하지 못한 병에 왕족들이 걸렸을 때는 궁궐 밖에서 소문으로만 널리 알려진 신비한 명의를 데려오는 일도 맡아서 해야만 했다. 어찌 되었거나 손을 쓸 수 없어서 왕족에게 불미스러운 일이 생겨서는 안 되었다.

Keyword - 모든 문제(병)에는 해답이 존재한다. 다가올 사건을 위해선 평소에 준비하는 자세가 필요하다. 여러 방면에서 다양하게 준비하지 않으면 안 된다. 전문적인 지식이 필요함. 지식에서 그치지 않고 실제 적용 가능한 분야에서 매우 발전하게 됨. 남을 위하는 일에서 특출난 재능 발휘.

54

32. PALACE NURSE MAKING MEDICINE

의녀가 약탕기를 달이며 부채질을 하고 있고 문 뒤
에는 뭔가 다른 의중을 가진 또 다른 의녀가 훔쳐보
고 있다. 왕족을 위한 귀한 약을 달이고 있는 의녀는
집중하느라 뒤쪽의 의녀를 전혀 의식하지 못하고 있
다. 정성스럽게 숯불의 세기를 조절하여 약을 달이는
일은 한시도 눈을 떼지 못할 만큼 중차대한 일이었다.
그렇기에 늘 마음을 놓을 수 없었지만, 사람이 하는
일이니 실수가 없을 수는 없는 법. 잠시라도 다른 생
각을 하다간 약이 타버릴 수도 있었기에 그 앞을 떠
나지 않고 지켜봐야만 했다.

Keyword - 잠시도 한눈을 팔아서는 안 되는 일.
잠깐의 방심이 화를 부르게 될 수도 있다. 오랜 시간
공을 들여야 성공할 수 있는 일이다. 물론 그러한 정
성이 꼭 효과가 있다는 보장은 없다. 그러나 해야만
하는 임무이고 완수해야 한다. 남을 위한 헌신. 또는
그러한 직업.

33. PALACE LIBRARY

조선 시대 왕실 도서관이자, 학술과 정책을 연구하는 기관이며 지식의 총체이다. 정책 수립과 왕명에 부합되는 여러 자료를 만드는데 핵심적인 역할을 했다. 많은 두루마리와 책자들이 얹힌 선반이 보인다. 심각한 표정으로 문서를 꾸미는 학자의 얼굴에 책임감과 긍지가 엿보인다. 많은 공적이 여기에서 시작되었고 후세를 위해 보관되었다. 따라서 이곳에 근무하는 관리들은 매우 조직적이고 지성적이지 않으면 안 되었다. 갑자기 어떤 문서를 찾아오라는 왕명이 하달되면 무엇보다 신속하게 움직여야 했고, 화재로부터 종이 문서를 지키는 일에도 안심할 수 없었다.

Keyword - 하나씩 쌓아 올려야 하는 일, 또는 그러한 일들의 총체, 지식과 관련이 있다. 육체적인 행위보다는 지성적인 일로 그 업적이 평가된다. 생각을 신중하게 하지 않으면 모든 게 제자리걸음이 될 뿐이다. 남이 해놓은 일에서 어부지리로 이익을 얻을 수도 있다. 학문의 운에 길함

34. TORMENTED AND ANGUISHED

궁궐 한적한 곳의 연못가에서 비단잉어를 보며 한숨짓는 궁녀. 나이가 어느 정도 되어 보이는 궁녀는 어릴 때 들어와서 지금껏 갇혀 지내는 세월이 마치 잉어와 같은 것처럼 신세 한탄을 하는 표정이다. 그 옆의 강아지는 아무것도 모른 채 마냥 즐겁게 궁녀 옆에서 아양을 부리고 앉아있다. 저 멀리 꽃 핀 나무들이 부질없이 시들어가는 궁녀의 청춘과도 같다. 이제 그녀는 좋았던 젊음의 나날이 다 흘러가 버렸고 궁궐 안에서 시들어가는 자신의 남은 나날을 헤아려 볼 뿐이다. 별다른 뾰족한 수도 없지만 외로움을 견디기에는 궁궐 안의 생활은 너무나 단조롭기 짝이 없다.

Keyword - 남모르는 한숨. 자신의 처지와 전혀 다른 존재들이 한자리에 모임 소통되지 않는 나만의 고민. 한정된 공간을 벗어나지 못하는 답답함. 작은 고민을 해보지만 결국은 제자리로 돌아와 있을 뿐이다. 그저 그런 생활 속의 고민. 큰 틀에서는 변화가 없는 생활. 외로움.

35. CORRUPT OFFICIAL

욕심 많은 표정의 관리가 가마에 올라서 조정에 나아가는 중이다. 가마꾼들은 힘겨운지 표정들이 좋지 않다. 그것을 아는지 모르는지 살찐 관리는 느긋하기만 하다. 의관의 형태로 보아 그다지 높은 벼슬도 아닌 것 같지만 자기가 쟁취한 자리가 매우 의기양양하고 마음에 드는지 잘난 척하는 표정을 숨길 수 없다. 가마꾼들이 작은 실수라도 한다면 가만두지 않을 기세이다. 어느 날 갑자기 좋은 기회를 손에 거머쥐어서 돈을 주고 한 벼슬일 수도 있을 터이다. 신분제가 엄격한 시절이었지만 예외는 늘 존재하는 법이어서 뇌물을 주고 신분 상승을 하는 이들이 꽤 많았다. 나라에서도 이것을 일일이 감찰하기가 어려웠다.

Keyword - 작은 이동수가 있다. 짧은 이동이지만 힘에 부치는 일이 될 수도 있다. 남을 모시게 되는 역할을 하던지 내가 남의 수발을 받게 될 수도 있다. 지금은 처해진 일을 완수해야 한다. 사람마다 자기만의 역할이 있다. 한시적으로 자기에게 처해진 것을 해내야만 하는 운명이다. 그러나 길진 않다.

36. PALACE ATTENDANTS ON NIGHT WATCH

밤에 궁녀와 내시들이 손에 등불을 들고 침전 복도를 걸어 다니며 불침번을 도는 것을 순라라고 한다. 도둑과 화재를 예방하기 위해서 행해지는 일이며 밤에도 낮과 마찬가지로 만전을 기해야 했다. 왕족들은 이러한 보호가 있었기에 깊은 밤에도 편안한 잠을 이룰 수 있었다. 이에 만일에 하나의 착오라도 있게 된다면 왕족들의 안전이 큰 위험에 처할 수도 있었다. 대부분 궁궐은 목조건물이었기 때문에 화재에 매우 취약했고 한번 불이 붙으면 수습하기가 매우 어려웠다. 또한 왕족들은 반대파들로부터의 위험에 조심해야 했고 궁궐은 너무나 넓었기에 자객의 침입에도 늘 조심해야만 했다.

Keyword - 내우 주의를 기울일 일이 생긴다. 정기적으로 행해지고 있는 일에서 이상이 없는지 잘 살펴보아야 한다. 평온하게 주어진 오늘날은 누군가의 배려와 희생에서 비롯된 것이다. 내가 모르는 사람들로부터 보호를 받음. 구석구석 누군가 살피고 있음을 기억해야 한다.

37. CONSPIRACY

약탕기에 무엇을 넣고 있는 누군가의 손, 약의 성분을 더 좋게 하기 위해서 약재를 추가하고 있는 것인지 아니면 약을 달이는 누군가가 의도적으로 독을 넣고 있는 것인지 알 수 없다. 얼굴이 없는지라 누가 어떤 일을 하고 있는지 정확하게 알기가 어렵다. 음모를 꾸민 자를 잡아내기 어렵거니와 추측하더라도 증거가 없어서 난관에 처하게 된다. 이 시절에는 왕족이 죽으면 부검을 한다든가 하는 것은 상상할 수도 없는 일이어서 그대로 묻히는 경우가 허다했는데 그렇기에 독약으로 인한 피해는 헤아릴 수 없이 많았다. 왕족이라고 해서 비껴갈 수 있는 문제가 아니었다. 게다가 왕족은 자신들이 직접 음식이나 약을 만들지 않았기에 더욱더 그러한 위험에 노출되어 있었다.

Keyword - 감춰진 위험. 누군가가 나를 중상모략하거나 해칠 음모를 꾸미고 있다. 매우 조심해야 할 상황이다. 병점을 본다면 좋지 않은 결과가 예상된다. 주모자를 알 수 없는 일들이 벌어진다. 가장 가까운 사람을 경계해야 한다. 그러나 당분간은 누가 나에게 해를 끼칠지 알 수 없다.

38. INCOGNITO KING

평범한 옷차림을 하고 시장을 돌아다니는 왕과 그
의 수행원의 모습이다. 때는 한겨울이라 처마 끝에
고드름이 달려있다. 백성들의 삶을 돌아보는 왕의 얼
굴이 매우 심각하고 수행원은 혹여라도 닥칠 위험이
있을지 긴장하고 있다. 왕은 평범한 옷차림을 했지
만 고귀한 신분임을 숨기기 어렵다. 왕은 궁궐의 화
려한 생활과 비교해 백성들의 고초를 눈으로 목격하
고 적잖은 충격을 받은듯하다. 태어나면서부터 궁궐
을 벗어난 적이 없는 젊은 왕은 이제서야 실제를 목
격하고 자신이 받은 교육이 전부가 아니었음을 실감
하게 될 것이다.

Keyword – 낯선 장소, 다른 역할을 임시로 행해
야 한다. 뜻밖의 지혜을 얻거나 정부를 알게 된다. 한
시적인 변화이지만 꼭 필요한 변화이다. 근본적인 문
제를 알아야 한다. 귀로만 듣던 이야기를 직접 눈으
로 확인하게 됨. 상상 속의 정보가 비로소 실제로 다
가온다.

39. KING'S CHIEF SECRETARY

고심에 찬 왕의 명을 받은 현실 비서실장 도승지가 비밀 편지를 챙겨서 방을 빠져나오고 있다. 아마도 왕의 밀서일 것 같다. 왕은 아무도 의지할 곳이 없는 상태에서 외로운 결정을 내려야 하는 상황인 듯하고 비밀스럽게 도승지는 어명을 받들기 위해서 분주하게 길을 나선다. 그의 표정에서 지존인 왕과 하나의 마음으로 뜻을 이루고자 하는 비장함이 엿보인다. 왕은 최고의 자리에 앉아있었지만 그렇기에 자신의 의지를 내비칠 사람 또한 주변에 만치나 않았다. 아내인 왕비라고 하더라도 자신과 정치적 성향이 다른 집안의 딸인 경우에는 대화를 나누는 데 한계가 있었기 때문이다. 얽히고설킨 이해관계로 인한 불편한 심기를 가장 잘 살펴주는 것은 가까이에 있는 신하 도승지뿐일지도 모르겠다.

Keyword - 한마음으로 일을 행함. 어려운 가운데서도 도움의 손길이 있다. 나보다 지위나 나이가 어린 사람으로부터 도움을 받는다. 은밀하게 이루어지는 일. 충성심을 중요하게 여겨야 한다. 단순한 이해관계로 판단할 수 없는 매우 결속이 깊은 사람들의 만남. 또는 그러한 일의 진행

40. THE PRIME MINISTER

왕의 다음으로 가장 품계가 높은 최고직, 일인지상
만인지하의 존재이며 명예와 권력을 한 몸에 다 지니
고 있다. 희끗희끗한 수염과 관복에서 관록과 백전노
장의 기세가 엿보인다. 지나가는 관리들이나 궁인들
이 예를 표하고 있지만, 못내 무엇이 못마땅한지 어디
론가 눈길을 주고 있는 모습이다. 물론 그가 원한다면
거의 모든 것을 손에 넣을 수 있으리라. 하지만 이 자
리를 지키기 위해선 정적을 잘 다스려야만 했기에 긴
장 상태를 완전히 벗어나기는 어려웠다. 그것은 왕의
입장도 마찬가지였을 것이고 영의정 또한 그러했다.
모든 권력의 공통점이다.

Keyword – 모든 것을 다 누리고 있는 최고의 상
대. 매우 대길하지만, 자칫 교만해짐을 경계하라. 앞
길에 탄탄대로. 사람들의 존경을 받을 일이 생김. 자
신의 지위를 한껏 자랑하고 드러낼 기회가 생긴다. 긴
부귀영화나 그와 맞먹는 기회나 행운이 기다린다. 공
고한 권력과 위치.

41. UNDERCOVER ROYAL INSPECTOR

왕은 궁궐 내에 머물러 있는 날이 많았기 때문에 관리들이 궁 밖에서 어떻게 일을 하는지 제대로 알기 어려웠다. 그러기에 암행어사를 보내어 이들의 죄상을 기습적으로 확보하고 처벌하는 것으로 민정을 살피고자 했다. 평범한 선비 복을 입었지만 바람에 들추어지는 도포 자락 아래에 어사의 마패가 드러나 있다. 저 멀리 주연을 벌이며 취해있는 탐관오리들을 향해 나아가는 암행어사를 막아서며 개 한 마리가 사납게 으르렁대고 있다. 개마저도 탐욕스럽게 보인다. 그 나물에 그 밥이라고 봐야 하겠다.

Keyword – 드러나지 않고 일이 진행되거나 그러한 인물. 스파이. 첩자의 의미도 있다. 심상치 않은 인물이므로 외모로 평가해서는 안 된다. 결과가 늦어지는 감이 있지만 들이닥칠 때는 번개보다 빠르다. 안하무인인 아랫사람과 맞닥뜨리게 된다. 자신의 임무를 완수해야 하는 여정. 믿음직한 사람

42. BRIBE

궁궐의 문을 지키는 관리들과 각종 물품을 반입하
는 사람들 사이에 밀거래를 하거나 돈을 주고받는 장
면이다. 몰래 남의 눈치를 보는 두 사람으로 보아서
떳떳한 일은 아닐 것이다. 만일 윗사람에게 걸리게 된
다면 곤장을 맞을 일인지도 모른다. 수레에 실린 짐이
무엇인지는 정확하지 않지만, 반입이 불가한 물건일
가능성이 높다. 궁궐 내의 물품 검수가 매우 엄격하게
관리된 것은 맞지만 사람이 하는 일이다 보니 실수도
있고 틈도 있어서 이러한 불법 거래가 종종 이루어지
곤 하였다. 또한 윗전의 명으로 외부인들이 몰래 궁궐
을 들어왔다가 나가는 수도 있었다.

Keyword – 검열, 검사를 받을 때가 되었다. 엄격
하고 공정한 일이 유첩된다 것으로 보이는 것과는 다
른 속셈. 남들의 눈을 숨겨가면서 이루어지는 거래.
암시장. 불법적인 일에 연루되어서는 좋을 게 없다.
그러나 나도 모르게 휘말려 들어갈 수 있으니 조심해
야 한다. 소탐대실.

65

43. CHIEF EUNUCH

비록 내시이지만 젊은 날의 풍파를 다 지나서 이제
는 내시의 우두머리 자리에 올랐다. 평범한 사람으로
누려야 할 것들을 포기하고 자신의 운명을 받아들여
이제는 궁궐의 일부가 된 내시가 마땅히 누릴 만한 자
리일 수도 있겠다. 내시들은 후손을 볼 수 없었기에
양자를 두기도 했고 나이 어린 내시를 자식 삼아 수발
받고 의지하면서 여생을 보내기도 했다. 상선 영감은
위엄 있게 자신의 방에 비스듬히 앉아 한쪽 팔을 괴고
어린 내시의 안마를 받고 흐뭇한 표정이다.

Keyword - 눈치 백단인 사람을 곁에 두면 매우 유
용하게 쓰인다. 센스와 눈치에 있어서는 최고봉이다.
그러나 진실로 믿을만한지는 의문스럽다. 고생 뒤에
누리는 잠시의 안락한 생활. 그러나 눈치를 봐야 할
사람이 존재하기에 최고의 권력을 쥐기는 어려움. 하
나를 내어주고 하나를 얻음. 일반적이지 않은 직업군.

44. CHIEF COURT LADY

큰방상궁이라고도 하며 후궁과 승은상궁을 제외한 모든 궁녀들의 필두에 위치하는 상궁이다. 중전이나 대비와 직접 대면을 하는 것이 가능할 정도 영향력이 막강하였으며 왕족들의 생활과 밀접한 연관성이 있었다. 궁궐의 안살림을 도맡아서 해야 하는 상궁이었기에 나름의 권세가 있었다. 경망스럽게 꽃병을 깨트린 젊은 상궁을 나무라는 제조상궁의 표정이 기세등등하다. 물론 그의 잘못이 아니라 훨씬 아래의 사람이 저지른 짓을 뒤집어쓰는 중일 수도 있지만 지금으로선 눈물로 감내하는 젊은 상궁이다.

Keyword - 잘못을 지적받을 일이 생김. 모면하기 어려운 상황. 코너에 몰려서 어찌할 바를 모르게 됨. 자신이 윗사람이라면 아랫사람을 지적할 일이 생기고, 아랫사람이라면 윗사람의 꾸중을 들을 일이 생긴다. 내지는 자신이 저지르지 않은 일로도 망신을 당할 수도 있다.

45. COURT LADY GRACED BY KING

왕의 승은을 입어 상궁으로 봉해진 경우를 일컫는
다. 평범한 무수리에서부터 모든 궁녀들은 왕의 여자
가 될 가능성이 있었다. 왕의 사랑을 받아서 팔자를
고치는 것은 궁녀들의 꿈이기도 했다. 왕과 동침을 한
다든가 자손을 낳게 되면 품계는 갑자기 높아지고 후
궁이 되며 자신만의 화려한 거처와 궁녀들을 거느릴
수도 있었다. 하지만 그러한 기회가 늘 있는 것은 아
니었다. 왕은 한 명인 반면에 궁녀는 많게는 수백 수
천 명에 이르렀기에 저마다 왕의 눈에 띄고자 노력했
다. 어쩌면 노력으로는 모자라 하늘이 내려준 기회가
있어야지 가능한 일이기도 했다.

Keyword – 신분이 다른 사람들끼리의 만남. 은밀
한 합의. 두 번 다시 오지 않을 행운의 기회. 귀인이
찾아오니 인생에 다시 없을 순간을 잡아야 한다. 작
은 믿음이 큰 결과를 낳는다. 겉으로 봐선 알 수 없는
사람들의 어울림. 생각 외로 유대관계가 탄탄한 사람
들끼리 만남

46. FOOD TASTER COURT LADY

왕의 수라상 음식에 독이 든 것인지를 살펴보는 임무를 맡은 상궁이며 왕의 끼니때마다 은수저를 넣어 감별하고 있다. 어떨 때는 자신이 먼저 맛을 보고 난 후에 왕에게 음식을 올렸다. 궁궐의 왕은 늘 독살될 경우를 대비해야만 했는데 음식에 독을 타서 서서히 병들게 하는 수법이 만연한 시대였기 때문에 기미상궁의 역할은 그 무엇보다 중요한 것이었다. 모든 권력을 쥔 왕의 자리를 노리는 자들은 많았다. 반역을 일으켜서 왕위를 빼앗는 것보다도 병사하는 것이 탄로나지 않을 수 있었기에 왕은 이러한 반역자들의 행위에 늘 주의를 기울이지 않으면 안 되었다.

Keyword - 일상 속에 숨겨진 위험, 또는 그것을 파악해야만 하는 임무 평범한 듯이 보이지만 그 이면에는 늘 조심하지 않으면 안 되는 사항이 있다. 돌다리도 두들겨보고 건너야 한다. 남을 위해 자신을 희생해야 할 때, 직업, 소명 의식. 무언가 의심이 간다면 꼭 검사를 해봐야 할 것이다.

69

47. SECRET LOVE AFFAIR

흐릿한 달빛 아래에 궁녀와 내시가 사랑놀이를 하고 있다. 남의 눈을 피해서 약속을 하고 만나는 듯하다. 외로운 궁궐 생활에 많은 궁인들이 서로 짝이 없이 생활해야 했기에 때로는 이렇게 자기들끼리 눈이 맞아서 정분을 나누는 경우도 허다했다. 내시는 값비싼 노리개를 선물하며 자신의 마음을 표현하고 있다. 이것이 발각된다면 목숨을 내어놓아야 할지도 모르는 위험한 일이다. 지엄한 궁궐 내의 법도가 우선이라고 하더라도 자연스럽게 오가는 정담까지 다 막을 수는 없는 노릇이었다.

Keyword - 남몰래 하는 사랑. 전혀 알지 못하는 사이에 마음이 오간다. 드러내놓고 만나기 어려운 상황이나 그러한 인연. 예상치 못한 로맨스. 조심하지 않으면 망신살이 제대로 뒤집어쓰게 된다. 비밀은 비밀로 영원히 간직하는 것이 좋겠다.

48. SECRET DEAL

달이 뜬 야심한 밤에 만나서 나이 지긋한 궁인이 젊은 궁녀에게 서찰을 쥐여주고 있다. 그들의 눈빛으로 보아 모종의 음모에 가담하고 있는 듯하다. 물론 그들은 자신들이 모시고 있는 윗전들에게 전달하기 위해 이런 모험을 감행하고 있는 것일지 모른다. 하지만 그것이 만에 하나 탄로가 난다면 죽음을 면하기 어려울 터이다. 자신들이 모시고 있는 사람들의 명을 듣지 않아도 죽고 왕에게 들통이 나도 죽을 수밖에 없었기에 신분제도에 얽매여 꼭두각시처럼 그들의 손과 발이 되어야만 했다.

Keyword – 자신의 역할을 충실히 수행하지만 되돌아올 위험도 생각해봐야 한다. 남이 알아서는 곤란한 비밀을 공유함. 음모와 책략. 탄로 나기 쉬운 시기니 각별히 신경을 써야 한다. 머지않아 탄로될 비밀. 완벽하게 믿음이 가는 사람은 아니지만 어쨌거나 지금은 같이 움직여야 함.

71

49. ROYAL MEAL TABLES

왕이 식사 후에 자신의 수라상에 많은 음식을 남기고 물려주면 궁녀들이 받아서 음식을 나누어 먹는 것이 관례였다. 왕이 물려주신 것은 무엇이라도 은혜롭게 여긴다는 뜻도 담겨있지만, 왕이 드신 후에야 아랫사람들이 밥을 먹는다는 의미도 있었다. 왕은 어버이와 같았고 어른을 공경하는 것은 효의 가장 근본이었기에 왕을 이와 동일시 하는 것은 당연한 일이었다. 물론 수라상에 올라가는 음식들이 너무나 고급재료였기 때문에 이를 맛보는 기쁨도 있었으리라. 왕은 궁인들이 이를 맛보기를 기다리는 것을 알고 일부러 넉넉히 남겨주는 아량을 베풀었다. 그러기에 궁인들에게 이 맛있는 음식을 먹는 것은 유일한 낙이 될 수도 있을 터였다.

Keyword - 뜻밖의 선물, 보너스. 위에서 아래로 흐르는 행운이나 복이 있음을 암시한다. 순종하는 미덕으로 인하여 많은 것을 하사받게 된다. 작은 상을 받거나 치하를 받을 일이 생긴다. 자신의 역할에 충실하면 의식주가 안정된다. 능력 있는 사람 옆에서 어부지리를 챙김.

50. SUNDIAL

맑은 날 태양이 떠오를 때 하루의 시간을 알기 위해 고안된 것이다. 해시계는 왕궁에 쨍쨍하게 해가 내리쬐는 곳에 설치되어 궁궐의 시각을 촘촘히 알려주는 기능을 했다. 하지만 흐린 날에는 그다지 소용이 없다는 단점도 있었다. 제시간이 되면 궁인들이 큰 종을 친다거나 해서 궁 안은 물론 도성에도 그 시각을 알렸다. 지금보다는 조금 다른 방법으로 시각을 알렸는데 현대의 시각이 한 시간 간격으로 이용되는 것이 일반적이라고 한다면 예전에는 12 지지를 기점으로써 알리기도 했다. 자시 축시 이렇게 알렸는데 이는 현대의 두 시간에 해당된다. 만약 인시에 만나자고 약속한다면 새벽 3시에서 5시 사이를 일컫는다. 예전 사람들은 이러한 기다림이 익숙했을까? 어땠을까?

Keyword - 순서대로 일이 일어남. 역전되는 것은 없다. 제대로 하지 않으면 재미를 보지 못한다. 작은 것이라도 질서 있게 진행해야만 한다. 모든 일에는 기한과 과정이 필요한 법이다. 한번 간 것은 돌아오지 않는다. 정확도가 요구되는 일을 하거나 그런 사람을 만난다.

51. TUHO, ROYAL WINTER GAME

왕족들이 비단옷을 입고 흥겨워하며 겨울날 투호 놀이를 하고 있다. 두 편으로 나뉘어 항아리에 화살을 던져 많이 넣는 편이 승리한다. 넓은 마당 복판이나 대청에 귀가 달린 항아리를 가져다 놓는다. 항아리에서 10보쯤 떨어져 항아리 안에 화살이 들어가도록 하는데, 들어가면 1점을 따게 된다. 화려한 듯이 보이는 궁궐에도 무료함은 존재했고 각종 놀이를 즐기면서 자신들만의 기쁨을 찾았다. 그림 속의 주인공들은 승부가 중요하지 않은지 마냥 즐거운 표정들이다. 먼 산에는 눈이 내리고 있고 한겨울이 되었음을 알리고 있다. 뒤로 보이는 궁궐의 담장은 위험으로부터 왕족을 지켜주긴 하지만 반대로 갑갑한 생활을 상징하고 있다. 무엇 하나 아쉬울 것 없이 보이는 왕족에게도 즐거움은 소소한 것에서 오는 모양이다.

Keyword – 겉으로 크게 보이는 일이더라도 실상은 그게 심각하지는 않다. 그저 지금은 눈앞의 게임에 집중하는 것이 좋겠다. 알고 보면 시시한 일이 될 수도 있다. 평범함 속의 비범함. 함께 하는 일에 의미가 있다. 망중한. 행복은 자기 찾기 나름이다.

52. YUTNORI, FOLK GAME

궁녀들이 한가한 때를 보내기 위해 윷놀이를 하며 즐거워하고 있다. 윷놀이는 정월에 하는 놀이로 남녀 노소 누구나 신명으로 놀이를 한다. 재미로도 하지만 원래는 농경사회에서 풍년 농사를 기원하는 소망이 담겨 있다고 한다. 윷판은 농토이고, 윷말은 놀이꾼 이 윷을 던져 나온 윷 패에 따라 움직이는 계절의 변 화를 상징해 풍년을 가져오는 것으로 여겼다. 또한, 하늘의 별자리를 축약하여 나타낸 것으로도 보았다. 궁녀들은 궁궐을 떠날 수 없는 운명이었기에 그 안에 서 자기들만의 오락거리를 찾아야 했고 어울리는 궁 녀들끼리는 자주 모여서 즐거운 놀이를 함께 했다.

Keyword - 소소한 행복. 평화로운 한 때를 보낼 수 있다. 거창한 것이 아닌 것에도 의미가 있다. 만중 한의 여유. 여러 사람이 함께하는 활동일수록 효과가 좋다. 위대한 무엇인가를 찾기보다는 흘러가는 대로 두는 것이 현명하다. 서로 잘난 척 해봐야 도토리 키 재기다. 그렇고 그런 사람들의 모임.

75

53. MISSING YOU

저 멀리 열린 창문으로 푸르른 나무와 하늘이 보이는 아름다운 풍경과는 대조적으로 후궁은 무슨 일인지 편지를 받아들고 눈물을 짓고 있다. 간만에 사가에서 가족들로부터 소식이 도착한 것일 수도 있다. 그 내용이 기쁜 것이든 슬픈 것이든 예전처럼 쉽게 가족을 만나지 못한다는 사실이 어린 마음에 사무친 것일 수도 모른다. 아직은 가족들과 함께 지내고 싶은 나이에 궁궐에 들어와서 엄한 규칙을 배우며 왕족의 일원이 되어가는 과정이 만만치는 않았을 것이다. 게다가 주변에 의지할 곳 없는 신세여서 늘 외로울 수밖에 없었다. 아름다운 비단옷으로 한껏 치장한 모습에도 불구하고 궁궐 밖의 가족을 그리는 마음은 여전하여 눈물이 흐른다.

Keyword – 소식이 당도한다. 반드시 좋은 소식이 아닐 수도 있다. 그러나 갑갑한 일은 일부 해결된다. 공적인 일보다는 사적인 일에서 결과가 빠르다. 그다지 나쁜 운이 아니니 참고 견디면 보람을 찾을 수 있다. 정해진 틀 안에서 역할을 수행해야 한다. 제한된 자유. 오래된 그리움.

76

54. PERFORM ANCESTRAL RITES

한나라의 왕과 왕비라고 하더라도 돌아가신 선왕에 대한 제사는 친히 지내러 가야 했다. 아무리 세상의 지존이라고 하더라도 부모와 자식의 도리를 지켜야 함은 백성과 다르지 않았다. 모든 것의 근본은 효성이기 때문이고 이를 통해서 백성을 다스렸기 때문이다. 멀리 왕묘가 보이는 곳을 향해서 지어진 제실에서 제수용품을 진열하고 있다. 선왕의 무덤은 살아있을 때의 옥좌와 같이 높은 곳에 잘 안치하였고 저 멀리 떨어진 제실에서 그 풍경을 보면서 제사를 올리도록 하였다. 일정 거리를 두고 이렇게 지어진 이유로는 선왕에 대한 존경을 바침과 더불어 신하와 백성들에게 왕조의 정통성과 위엄을 과시하기 위함도 있었다.

Keyword – 드물게 찾아오지만, 꼭 갖추어야 하는 예시. 매우 중대한 일의 진행에 참여한다. 규칙과 전통에 따라야 한다. 개인의 자유의지는 그다지 중요하지 않다. 윗사람의 의견을 따르면 행운이 온다. 가정 내에서 웃어른을 모시거나 극진한 대접을 할 일이 생긴다.

55. ROYAL KITCHEN

많은 궁인들이 소반을 들고 이리저리 움직인다. 분주한 가운데 뜨거운 김이 오르는 요리를 준비하는 이도 있고 정성스럽게 만두를 빚는 사람도 있다. 왕의 식사인 수라상을 준비하는 데에는 특히나 많은 인력이 소모되었다. 왕의 가장 기본적인 건강에는 매 끼니를 건강하게 챙겨야 하는 부분이 매우 중요했다. 그렇기에 늘 신선한 식자재와 전국에서 공수해온 특산물을 가미하여 제철에 맛볼 수 있는 산해진미가 준비되었다. 하지만 덕이 있는 왕은 가뭄이나 전쟁 등이 일어나서 백성들의 삶이 피폐해지면 스스로 반찬의 가짓수를 줄여 백성들과 함께 아픔을 나누기도 했다. 물론 과식을 해서 일찍이 당뇨병에 걸린 왕들도 많았다. 건강을 위해선 거친 음식이 좋다는 것은 현대에 와서 알려진 사실이니 아이러니가 아닐 수 없다

Keyword – 만찬이 준비된다. 실제 그러한 파티나 연회에 초대받을 일이 생긴다. 아니면 남을 위해서 내가 그러한 역할을 맡아서 준비해야 한다. 좋은 소식을 기대할 수 있다. 그러나 남의 잔치를 준비하기만 하지 정작 내 입장에서는 아무것도 소득이 없을 수 있다. 분주한 일터.

56. ROYAL GARMENT

왕이 입는 옷을 용포라고 한다. 노란 색, 또는 붉은 색 비단으로 지었고, 가슴, 등, 양어깨에는 보 라고 하는 금실로 수놓은 오조룡을 붙였다. 왕의 옷을 짓는 기관이 따로 존재했으며 여기에서 완성된 용포는 따로 관리하는 궁인이 있어서 늘 주름을 펴고 향을 입히는 등 갖은 정성을 들였다. 그림 속에 향로를 쥔 궁인은 이제 막 향을 올리는 모양이다. 용포는 왕의 존엄을 상징했으며 왕 자체이기도 했다. 나라의 단 한 명만이 입을 수 있는 절대 권력자의 옷이었기에 각별히 관리되어야만 했다. 왕실에서는 의복으로 지위고하를 나뉘었는데 그중에서도 단연 돋보이는 것은 당연히 왕의 의복이어야만 했다. 용포의 색깔은 시대마다 조금씩 바뀌기도 했는데 노란색이나 붉은색을 썼다.

Keyword - 내가 주인공이 아닌 일에 큰 기대는 금물이다. 어떤 결과를 기다린다면 아직은 시기상조이다. 일이 지체되며 수동적이다. 누군가 역할을 하기 전에는 움직일 수가 없다. 대세가 오기 전에 움직여서는 안 된다. 이동수에는 그다지 길하지 못하다. 시간이 걸리며 지체된다.

57. AMBASSADORS FROM MING

인접한 나라와의 관계를 외면할 수 없었던 왕의 관점에서 외국의 사신은 대하기 쉽지 않은 손님이었다. 그들은 자기네 나라의 이익과 지배자들의 생각을 전달할 목적으로 왕을 종종 방문하곤 했다. 그러기에 거만하기 일쑤였고 자기들이 한껏 대접받는 것을 당연하게 여겼다. 가마에서 내리는 사신 또한 뒷짐을 지고 먼 산을 바라보며 관리의 안내를 받고 있다. 못마땅한 표정에서는 벌써부터 무엇인가 꿍꿍이가 가득 차 있다. 그는 곧이어 왕을 알현하고 자신의 속내를 드러낼 작정이다. 물론 자신들의 입장만 내세우며 셈을 할 계획일 것이 분명하다. 만일 왕이 현명하게 대처하지 못한다면 사신의 무리한 조공 같은 요구를 받아들이게 되고 그렇게 되면 백성이 힘들어질 것은 정해진 수순이었다.

Keyword - 남으로부터 기분이 좋지 않은 지시를 받을 수도 있다. 먼 곳에서 오는 무리한 요구. 거절하거나 무시할 수 없는 상대와 만나야 한다. 예정된 만남. 적반하장. 연쇄반응이 되기 전에 기선제압을 해야 함. 각종 다방면으로 준비해야 함. 만전을 기한다고 하더라도 기습적인 요구를 하는 상대와 만남

58. REGIONAL PRODUCTS

전국 각지에서 궁으로 진상되는 특산물들이 차례
를 기다리고 있다. 관리들이 목록과 대조를 해가며 꼼
꼼하게 체크를 하고 있다. 왕실에서는 여러 가지 방법
으로 세금을 거두었는데 포목이나 쌀 등도 있었지만
지역의 우수한 특산물을 제철에 거두어들이는 것도
매우 중요한 일이었다. 개 중에는 너무나 무더운 날
씨에서 이송하는 중에 상해버리는 음식도 대단히 많
았기에 매우 주의를 기울이지 않으면 안 되었다. 전
국의 산해진미를 모두 맛볼 수 있는 즐거움을 왕족들
은 당연히 누렸지만, 그것이 공수될 때까지의 어려움
은 결국 백성의 몫이었다. 덕분에 왕실은 고급음식과
문화를 누릴 수 있었고 그것은 결국 우리의 유산이 되
어 현재에까지 이르고 있다.

Keyword - 재물이 차곡차곡 쌓여감. 사업이 번창
하다. 지금으로선 나무람이 없는 생활이 보장되어 있
다. 검수와 검사가 필요한 시점. 장부 정리나 계산이
요청됨. 남의 재산이나 재물을 감독하고 관리해주는
역할자. 이동하는 동안 주의가 요청됨. 물자가 풍부
한 환경

59. JOSEON MISSIONS TO JAPAN WELCOMED

일본 항구에 조선의 왕실에서 파견된 배가 닻을 내리고 있다. 뱃전에 서 있는 관리는 오랜 시간 항해를 마치고 드디어 목적지에 닿은 보람을 만끽하고 있고 은은한 미풍이 불어오고 있다. 항구에는 조선에서 온 사절단을 보기 위해 일본의 귀족들이 속속 모여들고 있다. 조선 국왕으로부터 일본 장군에게 파견된 인원들은 매우 다양하였고 많은 문물이 이때 교류되었다. 일본 국왕의 길흉 또는 양국 간의 긴급한 문제를 해결하는 목적을 갖는 만남인 만큼 왕족과 더불어 귀족들의 문화에도 지대한 영향을 끼쳤다. 조선의 왕이 일본의 왕에게 전달할 국서와 예단을 함께 갖추고 통신사들은 일본 땅을 밟았으며 일본 또한 극진한 예로써 이들을 맞이하였다. 1600년대부터 근 200년가량 12회 방문하였으며 그 일정은 매우 길고 화려한 이야기를 낳았고 일본 전국을 순례하며 다양한 문화적 교류를 가능하게 하였다.

Keyword - 멀리 출장을 가거나 이동할 일이 생김. 멀리 갈수록 이로운 일과 명예가 함께 한다. 낯선 곳에서 좋은 일이 생긴다. 새로운 것을 접해야 할 시기. 계속 머물러 있어선 좋은 것이 없다. 다른 사람을 대신해서 심부름할 일이 생김. 단체로 움직이는 일에 길함.

60. JOSEON MISSIONS TO JAPAN RECEPTION

통신사들이 긴 여독을 풀기 위해 잠시 한가한 시간을 보내고 있다.. 편한 옷차림으로 갈아입고 귀족들의 저택을 방문한 듯 보인다. 뒤로 일본 막부의 문양이 들어간 휘장이 드리워진 것으로 보아 최고급 관리임을 알 수 있고 앞에는 일본 특유의 회 요리와 술이 놓여있다. 통신사들도 이국에서의 밤을 즐기는 중인지 얼굴에 웃음이 만면하다. 이 시기에는 조선과 일본이 더 없이 우애 있게 교류하던 시기였기에 통신사들의 방문은 딱딱한 관례가 전부가 아니었다. 그들은 서로의 문화를 심도 있게 나누었으며 서로의 다름을 이해하고 존중했다. 또한, 양국이 이로 인해서 얻어지는 이익은 각계각층의 다양한 발전을 이루게 했다.

Keyword - 귀한 손님을 대접하거나 내가 대접을 받으러 갈 일이 생긴다. 특이한 경험. 미지의 행운을 접한다. 이국의 사람과 교제한다. 새로운 것을 접하게 됨. 망중한. 고생 끝에 약간의 호사스러운 휴식은 누려도 될 것이다. 격식 있는 사람들과의 교류. 풍부한 경험을 주는 여행.

61. FALLING BLOSSOMS ON FLOWING STREAM

　궁궐 뜰의 연못에 꽃이 떨어져 흘러가고 있는 것을 후궁이 바라보고 있다. 자신의 청춘이 꽃보다 아름다운 것을 모르는 것 같다. 아니면 꽃을 보는 것이 아닌 다른 생각에 잠겨 있는지는 알 수 없다. 다른 카드에서 늙은 궁녀가 연못가에서 잉어를 바라보며 한탄하고 있는 것과 다른 의미가 있다. 자유만 없을 뿐 사실 후궁은 왕의 사람으로서 모든 것을 다 누리고 살며 행운이 따른다면 왕비의 자리에도 오를 수 있었기 때문이다. 어쩌다 궁녀가 왕의 승은을 입어서 후궁의 신분으로 격상되는 일이 있긴 했지만 거의 드문 경우였고 후궁은 왕비가 후사를 보지 못한다든가 다른 이유로 해서 명망 있는 집안의 여식이나 매우 아름다운 재인이어야만 그 후보가 될 수 있었다. 아무튼 아름다운 시절임은 틀림이 없다.

　Keyword – 자신이 알아차리지 못하는 행복. 배부른 한탄. 어쨌거나 주어져 있는 행복과 운명. 잠시의 일탈. 사람들의 이목을 주의해야 한다. 구설에 오를 수 있으니 조심할 것. 남에게 나의 행복이나 불행을 쉽게 떠들어놓아선 안 될 것이다. 나도 모르게 부러움의 대상이 된다.

62. TURTLE SHIP

임진왜란 직전에 이순신 장군이 건조하여 왜군에게 큰 타격을 주었고, 세계 최초의 돌격용 철갑전선으로 평가된다. 바다에 번개마저 치고 있는 상황에서도 거침없이 앞으로 돌진하는 거북선의 위용은 천하에 두려울 것이 없는 기개를 펼쳐 보이고 있다. 바다의 영물인 거북의 형상을 본떠서 만들었기도 했지만, 세계 어디에서도 보기 힘든 특이한 형태로 매우 인상적이다. 한국은 삼면이 바다에 접하였기에 해상왕국으로서 거북이처럼 바다의 길을 훤히 알고 해상전투에 능한 자부심을 표현하기에 부족함이 없는 모습이다. 칠흑 같은 밤에 풍랑이 심하게 일고 있다. 하지만 거북의 얼굴은 꺾이지 않은 채 앞을 주시하며 나아간다. 물론 배 안에는 그보다 더 용맹한 장수와 군인들이 노를 젓고 있을 터이다.

Keyword - 보이지 않는 것을 본다. 신묘한 능력. 머물러 있어서는 손해를 본다. 위기의 상황이 반전을 가져오려면 대단한 용기가 필요하다. 판단력이 요구되는 시기. 잦은 이동 속에 많은 변화가 있다. 여러 사람의 말을 믿지 말고 자신만의 신념을 지켜야 한다. 환경에 지배되지 않을 투철한 정신.

63. JAGYEOKRU

세종대왕의 명으로 장영실 등이 만든 물시계이다. 스스로 시각을 알리기 위해 고안된 장치로 물의 양이 차면 인형 3구가 종과 북과 징을 치게끔 고안되었다. 그림 속에는 더욱 정교한 시각을 맞추기 위해서 관리가 점검하고 있다. 시계의 기능은 단순히 정확한 시간만 안다는 것에 그치지 않았고 절기를 제대로 아는 것에 까지 이어졌다. 절기를 안다는 것은 농사와 직결되었고 당시에 농사는 한 나라의 운명을 좌지우지할 만큼 중차대한 문제였다. 또한 실리적인 문물이 계속해서 개발되고 발전되기 위해서는 왕가의 지원이 필수적이었다. 지혜로운 왕이 다스리는 시기에는 이렇듯 모든 것이 꽃처럼 피어났고 재능 있는 자들이 진출하여 저마다의 솜씨를 뽐낼 수 있었다.

Keyword - 이론만이 아닌 실제적인 기술이 필요함. 그와 맞는 일을 선택하면 좋은 결과가 있다. 탁상공론은 의미가 없다. 유력한 사람의 지원을 받는 일. 널리 알려지는 일이면 더 좋은 기대를 해볼 수 있다. 작은 목적보다는 대의를 위해서 행함이 이롭다.

64. METAL TYPE

세계 최초의 금속활자인 직지심체요절의 준말로 줄여서 직지라고도 한다. 이 책은 19세기 말 대한 제국의 마지막 시기에 프랑스의 초대한국공사인 콜랭 드 블랑시라는 사람이 정식으로 구매한 것이며 이것이 몇 단계를 거쳐 나중에 프랑스 국립도서관으로 흘러 들어가게 된 것을 후일 박병선 박사가 그곳에서 사서로 일하면서 발견하게 되는 긴 여정을 거쳤다. 이후에 유네스코가 지정한 세계기록문화유산 가운데 해당 국가에 있지 않은데도 선정된 유일한 예가 되었다. 금속활자의 발명은 인류 역사에 지대한 영향을 끼쳤는데 이전에는 양피지에 필사하는 것이 유일한 방법이어서 많은 사람에게 지식을 전달할 수 없던 것에 비해 인류의 문화를 비약적으로 발전시킬 수 있는 획기적인 전환점이 되었다. 그림 속에는 또 다른 책을 인쇄해보는 장인이 매우 긴장된 표정이다.

Keyword - 언론이나 확대 재생산되는 소문들. 또는 정보. 규격화되는 일일수록 적성에 맞다. 작은 아이디어에서 큰 보람 있는 결과를 얻을 수 있다. 시작은 작은 생각에서 출발한다. 남을 위해 헌신하는 직업. 그러한 역할을 할 때 의미가 있다. 혼자 알고 있는 일은 재미가 없다.

65. TREASON

역대 왕들은 언제나 반역을 두려워해야 했다. 그 대상자들은 왕이 될 비슷한 서열의 형제이거나 또는 종친이거나 다수의 이익에 관련된 자들 중의 하나가 주동하거나 하였다. 다양한 방법으로 역모가 시도되었고 일부는 실제로 성공해서 왕좌에 앉기도 했으며 이에 몰락한 왕은 대부분 비참한 최후를 맞이할 수밖에 없었다. 왕권은 하늘이 내린 것으로 백성들에게는 알려져 있었지만, 실제 최측근에서 권력을 잡고자 벌이는 암투는 상상을 초월할 만큼 비정하며 인간이기를 거부하고 최종적으로는 인륜과 천륜마저 저버리는 경우가 빈번했다. 밤에 횃불을 들고 모여든 무사들의 음산한 분위기에서 폭풍전야가 느껴진다. 이들의 음모가 성공할지 어떨지는 미지수이다. 그들에게는 지금 눈앞의 거사를 성공시키는 것만이 중요할 뿐이다.

Keyword – 자신의 생각에 갇혀 있기에 옳고 그름을 따지는 것이 불분명하다. 목적과 대상이 분명치 않기에 절제가 필요하다. 휩쓸아치는 사람들과 일하게 됨을 경계하라. 내가 지위가 낮다면 결정권이 없으며 지위가 높은 사람이라면 후에 책임질 일을 진행해야 한다. 매우 위험한 모험.

66. ROYAL SEAL

옥으로 만든 국새이다. 국권의 상징으로 국가적 문서에 사용되는 왕의 도장이며 왕 자체를 상징한다. 한번 왕명으로 나간 것은 되돌리기 어려웠다. 그만큼 신중한 판단이 필요했으며 국새가 찍힌 서류는 그대로 실행되어야만 했다. 교지라고 해서 왕이 내려준 서류를 대대손손 가보로 보관하는 이들도 많았고 현대에 이르러는 대단한 문화적 가치를 지니게 되었다. 옥새를 빼앗긴다는 것은 왕좌를 누군가에게 빼앗겼다는 것과 같다. 권력자의 힘은 명령이 얼마나 실행되느냐의 여부에 달린 만큼 국새는 곧 그것을 이행시킬 힘을 갖고 있는 상징물이었다. 많은 전란 속에 옥새가 도난당한 경우도 몇 번 있었다고 하니 과연 한 나라의 운명과 함께 하는 귀중품이 아닐 수 없다.

Keyword 매우 높은 상급 기관으로부터의 허가가 필요함. 요식행위 때문에 일이 지연됨. 결과를 맞이하기까지는 시간이 걸림. 연락이 지체된다. 내가 명령을 기다리는 입장이라면 수동적이게 되며 반대로 결정을 해야 하는 입장이라면 더 이상 미룰 수가 없게 된다. 공식적인 절차.

89

67. CONCUBINE PUTTING ON MAKEUP

매일 아침 일어나서 단장을 하고 있는 왕의 여인
이다. 향합 등을 경대 앞에 펼쳐놓고 나름대로 유행
에 뒤지지 않는 화장을 연구하는 모습이 지금과 다르
지 않다. 옛날에도 여인들은 자신의 아름다움을 위해
서 외국에서 들어온 각종 진귀한 화장도구를 사용함
은 물론 민간에 효과가 좋다는 비법까지도 사용했다.
그 시대에는 독성이 알려지지 않은 수은까지 이용해
서 얼굴을 더 아름답게 만들려고 했다는 사실은 여인
들의 미적 열망을 잘 보여준다. 잘 사는 관리들이나
세도가들의 여인들은 자신들의 젊음을 더 붙잡아놓
기 위해서 매우 안간힘을 썼는데 한때는 여인들의 사
치를 막기 위해서 나라에서 법으로 규제를 할 정도였
다고 한다. 그림 속의 후궁은 화장하지 않아도 충분
히 아름다운데도 불구하고 거울 속의 자신을 들여다
보는 데 열중하고 있다.

Keyword - 과유불급. 지나침은 모자람만 못할 수
도 있다. 자기 자신에게 집중한 나머지 주변을 돌아
보지 못한다. 나르시시즘. 지나친 자기애는 모든 것을
망칠 수 있다. 남의 시선을 의식하기에 바빠서 진정
필요한 것이 무엇인지 알 수 없게 된다. 남 앞에 나를
내보여야 하는 직업을 갖는다.

68. HYANGWONJEONG

이 정자는 조선 후기 왕과 가족들의 휴식처로 이용
된 궁궐 건물이다. 육각형 모양의 초석과 평면 그리
고 육모 지붕 등 육각형의 공간을 구성하여 비례감을
두었다는 점에서 역사적, 예술적, 건축적으로 가치가
높다. 작지만 여러 가지가 조화된 모습이다. 그 앞의
연못 위에는 단풍이 떨어져 있고 이제 막 해가 지는
지 하늘은 노을빛이 가득 차 있다. 천하를 다 가진 왕
이라 하더라도 잠시의 휴식을 위해선 그렇게 큰 공간
이 필요하지 않았다. 사람이 안락함을 느끼는 아늑
한 공간의 규모를 충분히 이해하고 지어진 건물이다.

Keyword – 쉬어갈 만한 곳. 여유로운 평화. 주인
공은 아니더라도 주변인으로서도 만족한 삶. 약간의
휴식을 자신에게 허락함이 좋다. 분주한 곳에서 벗어
나서 조용한 곳으로 삼시 이동한다. 비밀의 공간이 필
요함. 자신에게 이미 모든 것이 충분히 주어져 있음
을 알아야 한다.

69. KYEONGHOERU

궁궐 내에서 가장 아름다운 곳으로 가히 꽃으로 묘사되는 경회루는 태종 때에 지어졌다. 경복궁 서쪽의 땅이 습한 것에 착안하여 큰 연못을 파고 그 위에 누각을 지었으며 돌기둥에 용과 화초를 새겨 넣어서 물속에서 마치 용이 헤엄치는 듯한 장관을 연출하여 이에 탄복한 외국의 사신이 남긴 기록이 있을 정도이다. 그 이름이 지어진 데는 의미가 있는데 아무리 나라의 군주라고 하더라도 좋은 인재를 얻는 것이 첫 번째 조건이라 해서 군신 간에 덕으로써 서로 만난다는 것으로 경회라는 뜻은 거기에서 비롯되었다. 경회루에서는 나라의 경사가 있을 때 연회를 베풀기 위해서도 더 없이 좋은 장소였으나 단종이 세조에게 옥새를 넘겨준 비극의 장소이기도 했고 연산군이 흥청을 만들어 후대에 흥청망청이란 말의 시초가 된 곳이기도 하다.

Keyword - 좋은 일이 많은 반면에 마음을 소홀하게 하면 방탕할 소지가 있다. 전반적으로는 위엄을 갖추고 큰 틀을 만드는 일이니, 공적인 일에 매우 적합하다. 주어진 기회를 잘못 쓰게 되면 큰 뒤탈이 있다. 남 앞에 나서야 하는 기회를 잘 활용하면 좋다. 큰 상을 받거나 축하할 일이 생김

70. KEUNJEONGJEON

경복궁이 창건되면서 지어진 중심건물이자 정전이며 역대 국왕의 즉위식이나 대례 등이 거행되었고 조선 왕실을 상징한다. 매우 중요한 공식절차와 의식이 여기에서 다 진행되었으니 궁궐의 대표적인 얼굴이자 핵심이라고 보아야 할 것이다. 근정이라 함은 열심히 정치한다는 뜻이다. 예로부터 나라를 다스리는 왕에겐 부지런함이 덕목이었다. 왕이 자기의 권력을 누리는 것에 앞서서 백성의 편안함을 살피기 위해 쉬지 않고 일해야 함을 알려주는 뜻이라고 하겠다. 또한, 근정전에서는 외국의 사신이 올 경우에 연회를 열고 불꽃놀이도 하는 등의 국가적인 손님맞이 또한 이루어졌다. 한 나라의 자존심이라고 할 만큼 가장 화려하게 건축되었으며 왕과 나라의 체면이 걸린 국가적 행사는 대부분 이곳에서 행하여셨나고 한다.

Keyword - 모든 일의 핵심. 또는 중심인물을 상징함. 격식에 맞는 일에는 유리하고 사적인 일에는 그다지 도움이 안 된다. 어떤 직제, 체계 안에 이루어가는 일에서 유리함. 큰 행사를 치르는 편이 이롭다. 밖으로 표출되는 일을 할 때이다. 여러 사람의 이목을 받을 일이 생긴다.

93

71. CHANGKYEONGGUNG

이 건물의 터는 세종이 상왕인 태종을 위해서 지은 곳으로서 아버지의 만수무강과 평안을 바란다는 뜻으로 원래 이름은 수강궁이었다. 이후에 세월이 흐르면서 대비들을 위한 처소로 고쳐 지으면서 창성하고 경사스럽다는 뜻의 창경궁으로 이름 지었다. 따라서 정치와는 그다지 깊이 연관되지 않은 궁궐이다. 그러나 자연과 궁궐이 아름다운 조화를 이룬 곳으로 유명하며 창경궁의 정문인 홍화문 앞으로 옥류천이 흐르는데, 이 물은 산과 강에서 나온 좋은 기운이 흐른다고 해서 '명당수'로 불린다. 일본 강점기에 동물원 등으로 이용되는 수난을 겪었지만, 다시 복구하여 그 아름다움을 선보이고 있다.

Keyword - 전환점을 맞이한다. 다시금 부귀영화를 누릴 기회가 찾아온다. 큰 어려움 없이 복을 누리고 재물을 취할 수 있다. 보호를 받고 안정된 생활을 누린다. 은퇴를 생각한다면 좋은 시기이다. 활동에서는 제한이 있을 수 있다. 먼 길 여행이나 출장에서는 이롭지 않다.

72. INJEONGJEON

태종이 거처하는 또 다른 궁전이며 인자한 정치를
펼친다는 뜻을 갖고 있다. 그 내부에는 태평성대를 상
징하는 봉황이 그려져 있다. 태종 이방원은 왕위에 오
르기까지 피의 숙청을 단행하였고 많은 충신들이 그
시절 희생되었다. 이후에 나라가 안정되고 평화의 시
대가 왔으며 그의 아들 세종은 최고의 성군으로 불리
게 된다. 왕은 자신이 결정할 수밖에 없었던 과거를
생각하며 앞으로 이루어나갈 새 시대를 인자함으로
다스리고자 마음먹은 것일 수도 있다. 그의 뜻대로 이
후에 조선은 500년간 유지되었으며 그 기반이 이 시
기에 모두 틀이 잡히게 된다. 여러 왕의 즉위식이 열
리는 곳. 외국 사신을 맞이하는 등 나라의 공식 행사
가 열렸던 장소이며 바야흐로 봄이 오고 꽃잎이 휘날
리는 그림이 궁궐의 역사가 꿈을 함께 느끼게 한다.

Keyword - 큰 갈등 뒤의 해결책을 찾음. 예전과는
달라진 상황. 긍정적인 변화가 찾아온다. 일이 일단락
되었으니 그다음의 차례를 생각해보아야 한다. 마음
먹은 대로 일을 진행해도 좋다. 공식적인 일에서 여
전히 길하다. 공적인 자리에서 상을 받거나 발탁된다.

73. MOON JAR 1

궁궐에서 왕의 명을 받고 내려온 관리들이 뭔가를 의뢰하고자 서성거리고 있다. 이곳은 고급 도자기를 굽는 가마터이다. 도자기 장인이 마침 그릇을 빚을 흙을 자세히 감별하느라 관리들이 도착한 것도 눈치를 채지 못하고 있다. 좋은 도자기는 좋은 재료가 기본이었고 그다음에는 불의 온도였다. 모든 것이 표준화되어 있지 않고 장인의 감각에 의존하던 때여서 이러한 전문가는 매우 귀한 대접을 받았다. 이들은 스승에서 제자로 그 비법을 전수해왔기에 자부심 또한 대단했다. 때는 봄인 듯 사방에 꽃잎이 흩날리고 있다.

Keyword – 세상일의 기본이 되는 것에 집중해야 한다. 단계를 뛰어넘어 실행하는 것은 의미가 없다. 제자리걸음이 될 가능성이 있다. 전통을 따르는 것이 좋다. 예기치 않은 손님들의 방문이나 제안이 온다. 그러한 제안이 그다지 불리한 것만은 아니다. 충분히 수용 가능한 조건들.

74. MOON JAR 2

열심히 물레질하며 항아리를 빚고 있는 장인들의
뒤로 관리들이 미심쩍은 듯 들여다보고 있다. 물론 장
인의 신경은 온통 항아리에만 집중되어 있다. 손의 감
각을 이용하여 반죽하고 도자기의 기본적인 틀을 잡
는 아주 중요한 단계로서 약간의 호흡만 흐트러져도
안 될 만큼 조심스러운 과정이다. 애지중지 만들어가
는 모습이 사람의 인생과 닮았다. 누군가의 손을 거
쳐서 만들어지느냐에 따라서 작품이 될지 그저 그런
그릇이 될지 알 수 없는 점 또한 사람의 인생과도 같
다. 운명이란 때로는 자기 자신이 개척하는 것일 수
도 있지만 남의 개입으로 인하여 급격히 전환되는 경
우도 많기 때문이다.

Keyword – 정성과 땀을 쏟아야 하는 단계. 다른
잡생각이 들어서는 일을 망친다. 하나를 완성해야 그
다음이 있다. 욕심만 가지고는 성사되지 않는 일이
다. 자기 자신과 싸움에서 승리한다. 대회를 나가기
전에 실력을 갈고닦는 과정. 스스로 이해가 될 만한
일이어야 한다.

97

75. MOON JAR 3

이제 빚은 항아리를 가마에 넣고 불을 지핀다. 가마의 온도는 사시사철 계절이 다르기 때문에 오로지 장인의 감각에 의해서 이루어지는 일이었다. 붉게 달아오른 가마의 불꽃이 장인의 열정을 대변하는 것만 같다. 밖에는 어느덧 신록이 우거져있다. 여름이 온 듯하다. 그 무더위에도 아랑곳하지 않고 장인은 열심히 나무를 때고 있다. 가마의 온도를 잘 맞추어야만 원하는 도자기를 얻을 수 있을 것이다. 이제 남은 것은 시간이 해결해 줄 터이다. 그럼에도 그 앞을 떠나지 않고 장인은 서성거리며 마치 자식의 탄생을 기다리듯이 자리를 지키고 있다.

Keyword - 지루한 시간과 싸우는 인내심이 요청된다. 하지만 의미 없는 기다림은 아니다. 이제 곧 결과물을 눈으로 확인할 수 있게 됨. 이동수는 불길하다. 하나를 향한 마음과 정열. 지금이 아니면 안 되는 일. 사람을 상대하는 일이 아닐 수도 있다. 전심전력을 기울여야 하는 상황.

76. MOON JAR 4

가마가 식고 나자 장인은 항아리들을 하나씩 꺼내어 매의 눈으로 점검을 하고 있다. 미세한 금이 가진 않았는지, 기포가 생겼는지 등등 명작으로서 이름표를 붙이기엔 뭔가 하자가 있는 것들이 없는지 꼼꼼하게 살펴보고 있다. 하나하나 모두 자식 같은 도자기들이다. 하지만 자신의 기대치에 맞지 않는 도자기가 있다면 너무나 실망스러울 터이다. 아무튼, 하나씩 점검해가는 과정이 예사롭지가 않다. 사실 한 번의 가마에서 나오는 도자기들은 일부만 불량이 날 수가 없고 하나가 좋지 않으면 나머지도 거의 불량이 될 가능성이 컸다. 재료도 같고 불의 온도도 같았는지라 어느 것은 잘나고 어느 것은 못나게 될 수가 없었기 때문이다.

Keyword - 자신의 자존심에 맞는 일을 행하라. 타협할 수 없는 진실. 높은 명예를 위한다면 경솔한 판단은 금물이다. 자신에게 정직하고 떳떳해야 한다. 그렇지 않으면 나중에 후회할 일이 생긴다. 기술적인 일에서 두각을 발휘한다. 자신의 판단을 믿어야 한다.

77. MOON JAR 5

자신의 눈에 들지 않는 항아리를 모조리 부수고 있는 장인이다. 그는 울고만 싶을 것이다. 공들인 노력이 수포로 돌아가는 과정이다. 어디까지 진행되었는지 보러온 관리들이 귓속말하면서 혀를 차고 있다. 그들이 아쉬워하는 것보다 더 마음 아픈 쪽은 장인일 것이다. 그는 자식처럼 빚어서 구운 항아리들의 결과가 이렇게 될 줄 예측하지 못한 듯하다. 아무리 열심히 한다고 해도 만약이라는 것이 있기 때문이다. 지금껏 많은 작품을 내어놓을 때마다 그는 같은 마음이었을 것이다. 장인은 대충 나온 도자기는 결코 시중으로 나가지 못하게 했다. 이것은 자기의 명예가 걸린 일이기 때문이다. 어느덧 계절은 가을이 되었다.

Keyword - 과감한 결단이 필요하다. 지금 어물쩍거리면 낭패를 본다. 남에게 주도권을 넘겨선 안 된다. 자기가 한 일은 자기가 끝맺음해야 한다. 결자해지. 강한 마음을 먹고 돌파해야 한다. 남의 이목 따위는 신경 쓸 필요가 없다. 타인의 도움이 지금은 오히려 방해될 뿐이다.

78. MOON JAR 6

포기를 모르는 장인은 다시 한번 더 물레를 돌리며 도자기를 빚는다. 그의 표정은 한층 더 비장하다. 밖에는 결과를 기다리러 온 관리들이 이제 지쳤는지 앉아서 졸고 있기까지 하다. 단풍이 마당에 가득 내려 쌓일 만큼 시간이 경과되었다. 관리들의 재촉이 있든 불만이 들려 오든 장인의 귀에는 이제 아무것도 들리지 않는다. 그는 도자기를 빚으며 자신과의 싸움을 하고 있다. 세상이 어떻게 돌아가는지 계절이 어디쯤 흘러왔는지 전혀 관심이 없다. 그렇게 해야지만 하나의 완벽한 도자기가 탄생할 수 있는지도 모를 일이다.

Keyword – 일의 핵심에 도달한다. 모든 것이 무르익은 상태. 주관과 객관이 하나로 합쳐진 상황. 자신만의 세상으로 들어가야 한다. 고독한 싸움에서 승리한다. 넘이 볼 땐 겉으로 평범한 일상일지도 모르지만, 자신만이 아는 비범한 하루. 또는 위대한 책임감. 프로 정신. 고단한 일상

101

79. MOON JAR 7

장인은 이제 다시 두 번째로 가마에 불을 지피고 앉아있다. 불길에 비친 그의 얼굴은 세상을 달관한 도인의 표정과도 같다. 이제 그는 하늘에 운을 맡기고 자신이 온 힘을 다해 만든 도자기들이 잘 구워지기를 기도하고 있는 모양이다. 자신이 할 수 있는 것은 최선을 다한 것일 수도 있다. 어쩌면 그는 불길을 보면서 문득 지난 세월을 떠올리는 것일 수도 있다. 진정한 완성작은 자신의 삶에서나 자신의 분신인 도자기에서나 모든 것을 내려놓았을 때 비로소 작품으로 승화되는 것인지도 모른다고 생각하는 것일까. 그 옆에는 기다림에 너무나 지친 관리들이 아예 코를 골며 잠들어 있다.

Keyword – 이제 곧 결과가 드러난다. 해가 떠오르기 직전이 가장 어두운 법. 모두가 신경 쓰지 않고 잊어버린 일이 다시 되살아난다. 두 번째의 시도가 오히려 효과적이다. 마음을 조급하게 먹지 않으면 좋은 일이 생긴다. 오랫동안 공들인 일일수록 성공적이다.

80. MOON JAR 8

드디어 원하던 달항아리를 얻었다. 장인은 기쁨에 넘쳐서 도자기를 들고 만족한 듯 관리들에게 선보이고 있다. 이제 막 잠에서 깨어난 듯 관리들 또한 오랜 기다림 끝에 작품이 성공한 것이 믿기지 않는 얼굴들이다. 처마에는 고드름이 달려있고 이제 겨울이 왔지만 기나긴 노고 끝에 드디어 성공한 완성작은 여러 사람에게 그간의 고생을 깨끗이 잊어버리게 한다. 참으로 먼 여정 끝에 하나의 온전한 작품이 탄생한 것이다. 거저 얻어지는 것이 없다는 평범한 진리를 다시 한번 느끼게 한다. 쉽게 구할 수 없기에 더욱 귀한 것이다.

Keyword - 완성. 드디어 원하는 결과를 손에 넣음. 두 번째로 시도한 것은 반드시 성공하나. 오랜 염원이 이루어짐. 기술직인 완성. 대가의 반열에 들어서게 된다. 특이한 아름다움. 평범한 사람의 눈에는 들어오지 않는 고귀함. 안팎으로 만족스러운 일이 연달아 생겨남

81. MOON JAR 9

마침내 제작된 달항아리가 왕의 앞에 진상된다. 왕
은 이것을 만들어낸 장인을 직접 불러 그 노고를 치
하하고 금은보화를 내려주고자 한다. 너무나 흡족해
하는 왕의 표정에서 매우 수준 높은 심미안을 가졌음
을 알 수 있다. 아름답고 질이 좋은 도자기를 생산하
는 능력은 나라의 국격을 높이는 데 큰 역할을 하던
시절이었기에 현명한 왕들은 정사를 돌보는 것 이외
에도 여러 가지 분야를 지원하고 육성해 왔다. 특히
나 이 항아리는 소박한 듯 아무런 문양이나 장식이
달려있지 않지만, 결코 소박한 항아리가 아니다. 입
지름이 바닥보다 넓어서 항아리가 공중에 떠 있는 것
같은 불안정감을 의도적으로 구현했다. 초가지붕 위
에 떠 있는 달을 마음속에서나마 그려 볼 수 있게 하
는 것이다.

Keyword – 큰 행사에 나아가서 상을 받거나 인정
을 받음. 마지막 관문을 통과함. 어려운 시험일수록
더욱 유리한 점이 있다. 불가능해 보이는 영역에서
오히려 실력을 발휘하게 된다. 뜻하지 않은 선물을
받거나 귀인을 만난다. 명예와 재물이 함께 찾아든다.

104

82. MOON JAR 10

이 미묘한 달항아리는 이제 궁궐의 한쪽에 진열되어 드나드는 사신이나 외국의 귀빈들이 감상할 수도 있었다. 물론 더 귀한 손님들에게는 선물로 증정되기도 했다. 달항아리는 은은하고 신비한 광채와 더불어 몸통 가운데 부분이 약간 비틀어져서 외형이 완전한 좌우대칭을 이루지 못하는 불완전함이 더욱 질리지 않게 보이는 깊은 매력을 느끼게 했다. 보름달이 뜨면 소원을 빌던 우리 민족에게 있어서 달을 닮은 항아리가 탄생한 것은 자연스러운 이치일지도 모르겠다. 왕과 백성 모두 인생살이에 있어서 한 치 앞의 미래를 알 수 없는 불안함이 있지만, 오히려 역설적으로 거기에서 삶의 지혜와 아름다움을 찾고자 했던 염원이 탄생시킨 걸작이라고 보겠다. 이러한 우리 민족의 세계관이 모두 이 달항아리에 담겨있는 것이다.

Keyword - 더 넓은 세계에서 인정을 받게 됨. 널리 알려지는 것이 유익하다. 혼자만의 생각을 겉으로 드러내고 같이 나누는 때가 되었다. 옹졸하게 처신해서는 불리하다. 더 폭넓은 사고를 해야 한다. 타인들로부터 평가를 받지만 결국 좋은 결과를 낳는다. 겉모습으로 판단해서는 안 된다.

Manual

Card Manual and Keywords

1. FORMER KING

The aged former king is sitting in the palace and looking out at the distant mountains. He seems to be reminiscing on his glorious days. The mountains are covered with white snow just as the old king is with his gray hair. He can sit back and spend the rest of his life in peace but he still has some regrets. We do not know if he is looking back on what could have been or would have been done, or having a remorse on shameful things that happened in the past. He appears to be living a mellow life but no one knows what is going on in his mind. The former king is to live the rest of his life peacefully. He has accumulated wisdom and experiences but he does not involve himself in the state affairs anymore. Any king ought to know when to retire those who retire at the right time are bestowed with significant benefits, honor and peaceful rest. Even the king of jungle tigers looks for a shelter to rest in when it ages.

Keywords

Reminiscing the past. Time to face the reality. Time to resign or retire. Peaceful time in retirement. Clear hierarchy of things. Advantages gained by clear commands. Stories of an old man. The older king represents the highest authority but actually has very little power.

2. PAYING RESPECT

A day in the comfortable life of the former king, with guaranteed safety. He still maintains his dignity as the father of the current monarch with absolute power. His merciful and relaxed smile provides a glimpse into his comfortable life in retirement. There are scrolls of documents waiting for his approval although his approval is a mere formality. The king expresses his filial piety by paying respect daily to his father every morning. The former king probably had thought hard before he chose the current king as his heir to the throne among his many other sons. In Joseon dynasty the basic rule of the game was that the eldest son of the king becomes the crown prince and eventually the next king, but in reality there were many instances in which other princes revolted and created exceptions to this rule. Therefore, a peaceful succession of the throne must have affected the former king's status as well. We can tell from the former king's content expression that his intentions were realized.

Keywords

Paying respect, visits, contacts by subordinates (with power, wealth). Affluent living. But involved in a bit of systematic, bureaucratic and formalized routines. Duties that need to be observed in the midst of the busy life. Documents of formality. Advice from the superiors. Advice from an old man.

3. QUEEN DOWAGER

The fierce eyes of the old queen dowager provide a glimpse into her ambition and passion that she is the one in control. She plays a dominant role in commanding opinions in the palace, and managing governmental affairs; she's not retiring anytime soon. The book open on her desk appears to contain progressive studies. The flowers decorated in the white porcelain vase demonstrate that she has a classy pastime. Her experiences in assisting the king deep inside the palace have turned her into an old veteran. She seems to be telling the queen about her life stories of keeping the concubines in check to get to where she is now and the wisdom she has gained from such experiences. Women in the royal family were no ordinary mothers-in-law and daughters-in-law; they had to take part in politics as well.

Keywords

Help from a classy, older lady. Has to be on the lookout in the midst of a peaceful life. Must seek permission from someone. Meeting up with a very discerning person of insight. A superwoman who can successfully manage multiple tasks. Enjoy a green old age. What appears on the surface is not everything.

4. QUEEN MOTHER'S REGENCY

The intimidated young king is sitting in the front, with the queen dowager with a stern face sitting in the back behind the veil. The young king is a mere puppet. But there is hope that after enduring this difficult time, someday, he will become a real king. Of course, under the assumption that the queen dowager would be willing to retire. There is no other way out at this time. For the time being, the powerless young king will not be able to exercise his authority. The queen dowager may want to surround the king with her people and have the young king forever stay powerless with no discretion. Some of the kings of the Joseon dynasty did not live until their heirs became old enough to succeed the throne, in which case the queen mother sat behind the veil for regency.

Keywords

Must play a puppet for some time. Time for patience and endurance. Painful time that no one else would take notice. Appears fancy outside but no real substance. What appears on the surface is not everything. There is someone else in control behind the scene. Must serve multiple bosses. Dilemma/Predicament. Difficult to grow mature due to excessive intervention.

5. ROYAL AUDIENCE

Finally the king has ascended to the throne as he wished. The officials are bowing to him. The king is looking out in the distance as if he is foreseeing his honorable future. Behind him stands the Ilwoloakdo (the Sun, Moon and Five Peaks) painted screen, which symbolizes the authority of the monarch. This painting was used only in the Joseon royal court among all of Asia, particularly in the king's official space, as a metaphor for the deification of the king with insight into the whole universe and harmony with the nature. In fact, the king's daily life was very busy and complicated. While much of his time was devoted to governing the state affairs, the king also had to take care of the matters of the royal family, greet envoys and ambassadors, and mediate the conflicted opinions among his officials from various backgrounds. Maybe some of his subjects bowing to him are only interested in advancing their own interests.

Keywords

Cannot be happier now. Complete with power, intelligence and youth. Respected by many. Ascended to the highest position. The one who reigns all with such greatness and excellence cannot be compared to any ordinary people. Meeting with a respected person of authority. Those whose interests differ stand very close to each other.

6. QUEEN TAKING A STROLL

The fully adorned queen is taking a walk in the garden. She took some time to spend a leisurely time in the garden, touching a maple tree and admiring its beautiful colors. Everything is ripe and mature. The queen is in the best period of her life, as well as the flourishing trees in the garden that boast their most beautiful appearances in the whole year. The queen, as the lady master of all internal affairs, was responsible for arranging, directing and regulating the affairs of concubines and all other women in the palace. Therefore, rather than revealing her own tastes and preferences her biggest virtue lied in holding down any noise in the palace and helping the king focus on state affairs. Further, a queen who gives birth to a son would be in a very strong position and would truly become the lady of the best distinction and honor.

Keywords

Step up to a mature stage. The backdrop and the main character become one. Abundant, affluent, and everything is in harmony. Relaxing time off from the pressures of work. Take a short break to go out and enjoy a leisurely time. A short but refreshing rest. One is in his/her optimal condition and the surroundings are also very satisfying.

7. ROYAL WEDDING

The wedding of the king and queen is a culmination of splendors. In the background there is an Ilwoloakdo (the Sun, the Moon and Five Peaks) painting which symbolizes the authority of the monarch; the sun and the moon in the painting, which symbolize the king and queen, respectively, are today replaced with the real king and the real queen instead. It is the day on which a public announcement is made to the heaven and earth and to the people of the nation that the couple is now married and will open a new era. The king wedded a noble lady from a prestigious family of his time; his marriage was of course a result of political strategies. The king's opinion hardly mattered in the selection of his bride among several candidates. The kings usually got married after they ascended to the throne but occasionally they got married when they were the crown prince. It is so ironic that even when the king rules and governs everything, when it comes to choosing his own wife, his will is hardly reflected in the decision.

Keywords

Consensus, accomplishment, achievement. The bigger the contract, the better the business will be, and smaller matters may be less satisfactory. Lovers will see fruition and face a new turning point. Great union. Success in partnership. Matters that had turned their back on you will rapidly change their course and bear positive results.

8. COURT LADIES

Three court ladies, dolled up as much as they could, are sitting in the room and showing off their jewelries and hairpins to each other. They are gossiping about their superiors and rumors. They have no bad intentions, but the stories that leak from them can cause a great commotion later. In places crowded with people, gossips and troubles never cease. This scene is a perfect example of walls having ears. The jewelries and hairpins that these court ladies are bragging about are expensive items that they cannot afford with their own salaries. They probably received them as a gift from their superiors or obtained them via other means. As these court ladies usually come from poor families and enter the palace for money, they are easily bribed with these luxury items. It seems as though the shadow out there that is listening to their conversation forebodes the evil to come.

Keywords

Immature behaviors. Joys of commoners. Great misfortune caused by seemingly harmless gossips. Have to watch what you say. Walls have ears. Places with many people inevitably bring about gossips and troubles. Not much of a difference; meaningless comparisons. Birds of a feather flock together.

9. ARCHERY BY CROWN PRINCE

The crown prince is a son born to the king and the queen. However, he seems to be taking out his anger on the practice of archery in the backyard of the palace. The eunuch beside him studies the crown prince's face to see if he is angry. A startled bird on a branch flaps its wings at the sound of an arrow. Still, there are many arrows hitting the target, indicating that the crown prince is a man of conviction that pushes forward what he has decided to do. To become good rulers, the kings of Joseon to had to put knowledge and virtue before physical strengths and fights. Perhaps the king does not like the aggressive temper of the crown prince. While it is true that Joseon dynasty's first king Lee Seong-Gye ended the Goryeo dynasty by a military coup and founded Joseon, he wanted the succeeding kings to be of civil and benevolent nature, which ultimately became the tradition of the dynasty.

Keywords

Small ambition. Secretly planning for the future, but it is too soon to let the plan known. Have to endure this time on your own. Placed in a situation that you cannot tell others. Not much help from those around you. Not in a great danger but isolation. Cannot enjoy the good position you are in.

10. EMBROIDERY BY PRINCESS

The little princess is sitting with the window closed and is concentrating on her embroidery. She looks quite serious. Kids of such young age would just want to go outside and play, but she is mature and tries to live a life that suits her social status. She is very fortunate to have been born to the royal family, but the education and refinement required of her from such a young age is quite strict. Particularly, the life path of a princess is already laid out at her birth. She has to marry a man from a prestigious noble family that the royal family designates, and her in-laws will not really welcome her because they would be placed in an awkward position of having to serve their daughter-in-law as their superior. However, such marriage is also a great opportunity from them to raise their social status.

Keywords

Precocious. Can proceed calmly. A young but dignified lady. The period of learning and practicing. Some things need to be given up to maintain the status. No ordinary life and living. Of prestigious birth or family origin; has the kind of character and skills that suit the birthright.

11. PRINCE PLAYING TAG

The prince is playing with the court attendants in the courtyard under splendid autumn leaves. However, he is not seeing the jagged stone at this feet and he may trip over it. Of course he can avoid it too. However, if he tumbles, the precious prince will get hurt. In such event, the court attendants playing with the prince would get severely punished; for this reason those around him are already nervous. Despite his young age the prince is an extremely important person, who had to be afforded the utmost care. The prince and his brothers, except for the one and only crown prince, would have to live in an unknown fate, because they must not get in the way of the king or else they could be used by others who wanted the throne. The face of the prince shows no worries. He smiles innocently as if he is unaware of his fate.

Keywords

Crisis approaching even those who seem to have it all. Danger hidden in what appears to be safe. Danger could just pass by. May get in trouble by helping out others around you. May have to take responsibility for being careless. Mistakes made in immaturity.

12. SPY

The spy in receipt of a letter tied to a hawk's foot at the dawn is showing some meaningful expressions. With whom outside the palace he is exchanging messages is unknown but it is obvious from his discreet manner that he is certainly not acting for the benefit of the king. The palace is so big and filled with so many people that there is no way to test the loyalty of each and every one of them. There is also no infallible way to monitor them. In some cases, the one who was supposed to perform sur- veillance turns out to be a mole. The people of the palace would want to act according to their principles but more often than not they are just tools of their own superiors. Of course, they are promised, as a reward, wealth and ad- vancement in their status. However, nothing can remain a secret forever; so it is unclear whether their plots will succeed.

Keywords

Traitor is nearby. Things take place in a discreet man- ner, Premature. Plots that have not yet been surfaced. There is a suspicious one among low status folks. Things that are hard to unveil. Plot, scheme. Long-awaited news arrives. It is unknown right now which side will be more advantageous to take.

119

13. BIRTH OF PRINCE

The newborn prince is swaddled in silk. The king together with his father rejoice and both are elated at the solid future of the dynasty. Outside the window, the bright morning sun rises, boding that the baby will become a great monarch in the future. The prince is loved by two of the most powerful figures in the country and is promised everything. Although the throne was supposed to be guaranteed as a result of the birth, there were also many unfortunate kings who were pushed out from their rightful place in the whirlpool of history. The royal family without a prince was in a very precarious position as, unlike the modern times, the dynasty had to continue through the bloodline. If there is no prince who would become the crown prince, it is evident that in case of the sudden death of the king, divided factions would fight to make the one they endorse the next king.

Keywords

Something has just begun. Great first step forward. Journey starting from a promised position. May not be in full swing but a predetermined wheel of fortune. A big flow not affected by one's wishes. Fated relationship. An auspicious, happy event that would be communicated to others or others would congratulate on.

14. SHAMAN'S RITUAL

A shaman who was sneaked into the palace by a female member of the royal family is performing some ritual. The royal women sitting in the front are intensely praying for something. The possessed shaman with ferocious eyes is transmitting messages from the spirits. However, this ritual is not an officially approved event, but is rather a secret ritual. If caught, these folks can get interrogated or punished. The queen, concubines and other women of the royal family usually prayed for giving birth to a son or for the king's love. When some grudge or bad energy seems to be getting in the way of their wish coming true, a shaman was invited to resolve those issues. Deep inside the palace in the women-only quarters, if they could only have the court ladies keep the secret, they could from time to time perform these rituals without the king's knowledge.

Keywords

Trying to get things processed through an unofficial route. Releasing stress accumulated in the mind. Relying on the supernatural for things beyond one's capabilities. Disgrace if caught. Might have resulted from a resentful relationship. Long-waited wishes come true.

15. ROYAL PLACENTA CHAMBER

The common people had a folk custom of saving the umbilical cord when a baby was born; this was not different with the royal family. It was believed that the umbilical cord had some inexplicable magical power and potency. The custom of cherishing the umbilical cord, the by-product of the birth of a baby, is a long-existing tradition. The commoners would, upon the birth of their child, save the umbilical cord and then later burn it or flow it onto the water, praying to turn away bad luck in the conception of the next child. When a prince, who would become a high and noble king in the future, was born, they selected an auspicious site to bury his umbilical cord, magnificently decorated the site and treated it as a sanctuary. A butterfly sits on the stone that signifies a placenta chamber. The butterfly symbolizes the soul of the ancestors and this seems to indicate that the royal ancestors are also celebrating the birth of the prince. The nature surrounding the site is in full bloom, promising a bright future for the prince, as this place is not a gloomy grave.

Keywords

Glorious events are about to occur. The first step to a great start. Discreet meetings or promises, monumental events, or evidence of secretive people. Things proceed in an organized, sequential manner, under the systems of a large organization. A bureaucratic event that no one can dare to ruin or defame.

16. KING'S HUNTING

One can feel the vitality of the young king hunting on horseback. The king often deliberately led the hunt to impress his officials. There were occasions, of course, when the king led battles in a war, but that was a very rare case. During ordinary times, the king apparently hung out with high-rank military officials to impress them with his power and authority. However, these events took place only to the extent of the king's inclinations. Only the king could mobilize military as private armies were forbidden in order to centralize the king's power. There are armed men and people of high social status following the king from the back. Unfortunately, a large bear hides in the shade behind the tree, eyeing the group. Who will be sacrificed is unknown; it could perhaps be the bear that will be sacrificed. The king has no idea about this imminent threat, as he is completely immersed in hunting.

Keywords

Big movement. You have to be moving around for gain. However, watch out for unforeseen dangers. People respond favorably but in the end you may have to deal with it on your own. Expect to benefit from a long distance travel or business trip but still have to be careful about risks. Be careful as to not let things end up in vain or futility.

17. PROCESSION TO TEMPORARY PALACE

It is a huge procession of the king traveling to another palace. The majestic procession of the officials and the trumpeters marching together displays the great power of the kingship to the subjects. In this journey of temporarily leaving the main palace to travel to another palace, the king has achieved his political objectives of observing the commoners' lives and patrolling the local regions, as well as strengthening his royal authority. The wise king does not limit his presence only to within the palace but regularly mobilizes a large number of people and significant amount of money to provide interesting sights for his subjects, and also to proclaim his reign. This is such a remarkable political gesture, even by the modern standards.

Keywords

Will be moving to another place or experience a big shift that will change all the bases of current living. Long distance move, move to overseas, study abroad. Large-scale activities in which people move in groups can be more suitable. Can catch two birds with one stone. A hidden, real motive separate and different from the known purpose.

18. SIXTIETH BIRTHDAY

It is a very honorable moment for the elder of the palace. Not all members of the royal family lived a long life, so the celebration of one's sixtieth birthday was a very special occasion. The king's mother certainly was in her youth once. She probably endured unspeakable years since she entered the palace at a young age. Her time in the palace was not always pleasant and splendid; on many days she just had to swallow bitterness without being able to tell anyone. As if she is being rewarded now for having gone through all those painful periods, the king's mother has a joyous, reminiscent expression on her face. On the other hand, it may represent her pride for what she has achieved thus far. Her husband, the former king, ruled, and obviously her son too will eventually become the king.

Keywords

Big event ahead. Very gorgeous banquet. You may be invited to a classy gathering or may have to prepare for such. The heroine cannot just rejoice; she must earn it to deserve it. Anyway it is a joyous day. Will attract attention from others.

19. PLEAS TO KING

Unlike the irritated king, the treacherous official with a secret plan in his mind is slyly smiling as he is bowing to the king. Perhaps the plea was presented to the king in order to create trouble for the king. The king, who does not know this, is placed in a very difficult position. The official ought to work for the king but apparently he is only using the king for his own ends. The king has to discern who is on his side and who is not. Various factions constantly struggled for power in Joseon and this was like a persistent disease that was very hard to cure. It is no different now that it is important to stop factional strife and unite for the good of people. A tense-strained confrontation of the king and his official.

Keywords

Different positions from each other. Note that you have treacherous ones around you. A junior may revolt against his/her senior(s). Will be meeting someone who brings you trouble. Be wary of those closest to you. What appears on the surface is not everything. Someone who will end up harming you is near you.

20. ASKING FOR FORGIVENESS

This is a rite performed when a member of the royal family seeks forgiveness from the king. The seeker of forgiveness would kneel down on the ground without wearing any formal attire. This rite would continue days and nights until the king officially grants forgiveness. Sometimes the seekers of forgiveness would grow so weak that they would faint. Often, seeking forgiveness without wearing any fancy clothes as if being a commoner irritated the king more so that the wrong committed itself. The rules of the royal family were very different from those of commoners, especially with respect to the relationship between the father and the son. In the royal family, their relationship was dictated by the duty of loyalty to the king, as well as a son's filial piety owed to his father. Regardless of how great the crown prince is as a son, it could be a sin if he was seen disloyal to the king. Of course, there were those who would stir up trouble around them,

Keywords

Crisis encroaching a seemingly relaxed, composed situation. Watch out for lawsuits and/or bad rumors being spread out about you. Do not make it worse by acting foolishly. May have to take responsibility for someone else's fault. May have to swallow pride. A stitch in time saves nine.

127

21. DANCERS

On a moonlit night the king and his key officials are having a party in the pavilion. They are chatting and having a good time, watching the dancers dancing. However, the pensive woman in the front seems to have something else on her mind. She may suddenly pull out a dagger from her bosom and rush to someone. Or maybe she is thinking of her lover. Even at the same party table, those in attendance all have different things on their minds. Professional dancers, in preparation for palace banquets, constantly practiced and prepared for their performance. Occasionally they performed with performing groups from abroad. Even though the royal family lived in the palace, they enjoyed high-class culture and entertainment flowed in from outside the palace. Still, while enjoying such entertainment, they had to be careful not to be seen too excessive.

Keywords

Can get wasted if too excessive, but sometimes such entertainment/pleasure is necessary. Moderate use can help. People with clearly different stances are gathered in one place. Face the reality that you are not the central figure. What appears extravagant and gorgeous may only be a party set up for others with no practical benefits to you.

22. KING'S MORNING ASSEMBLY

The king sits with a stern face at the morning assembly and the officials are bowing to the king on their knees. Unlike the ordinary times, military officers are guarding the chamber. Perhaps the king is trying to pass a law over the opposition of his officials or punish disloyal officials. Or, perhaps, this is a scene where the king is trying to show the real monarch's power. Or, maybe, the wrongs committed by some of the officials are finally about to come to light here. The king is not a puppet that the officials used to be able to control anymore. After a long period of deliberation, the king has finally decided to pursue his own politics. If he does not do this, he would remain a puppet who only does as he is told to do.

Keywords

You will find out the result in the near future. Official documents are delivered. Unfavorable in private matters. The moment of decision has arrived and cannot be put off anymore. Must make a decision. Otherwise, others will dictate what is going to happen, or you will be put through a formal procedure.

23. ROYAL ANCESTRAL SHRINE

This shrine is dedicated to the deceased kings and queens. It is a Confucian royal ceremonial structure in East Asia, which architectural plan is very unique and distinguished. The building is admired by top-notch architects around the world. Its simple yet overwhelming atmosphere creates the sense of grandeur of enshrining the spirits of the dynasty. The structure functions to confer a sense of legitimacy and power to the dynasty and represents the dynasty itself. The kings of Joseon, from their youth, regularly visited this shrine and learned about their heritage and the legacies of their bloodline, and were constantly reminded to keep them in mind. Consequently, they also came to realize their destiny. They learned lessons from the achievements and life paths of their great ancestors enshrined here, feeling and bearing the weight of their footsteps and realizing that they too would eventually be enshrined here.

Keywords

Very powerful in abstract and not so realistic. Unfavorable for ordinary folks living a tough daily life but this may be a good card for someone with power or social status. The most central concept that dominates a person's mind. Past wealth and glory.

24. DEATH OF KING

The ritual of Gobok is a traditional funeral rite. Gobok is a mourning ritual of asking the deceased to return, missing them with sorrow. It is usually performed by the eunuch who served the king closely. The chief eunuch or the lower-ranked eunuch would take the garment that used to be worn by the deceased king to the roof of the palace building in which the king passed away, and shout three times toward north 'Sang-we-bok', meaning "King, please come back to the living." The king's mother or the queen would shout 'Jung-goong-bok' instead. After the eunuch on the roof performs Gobok and tosses the garment in the air, another eunuch under the building would catch the garment and carry it in a box to cover the body with it. They would then begin to mourn out loud which would in turn be followed by a public announcement of the death of the king. A new era with a new king will begin.

Keywords

Sad, but one era passes and a new one arrives. Better not cling to the past. Returns to where it came from. The hour of destiny is approaching. Goodbye has a meaning. The end of all great things. The big event comes to an end in the grand finale.

131

25. PLAY BLINDFOLD TAG

On a spring day with beautiful flowers in bloom in the courtyard, the young princess is playing blindfold tag with court ladies. In fact, it is the youth of the princess that is more beautiful than the flowers. She is able to lightheartedly enjoy her life, not only because she is not married yet, but also because she has no duties as those required of a prince. Princesses lived a comfortable life with guaranteed security and they were rarely deprived of their royal status. During the Joseon dynasty, social participation by women was minimal, and not many opportunities were given to the princesses in the palace, either.

Keywords

Unskilled beginning, but an affluent life with almost all needs and wants fulfilled. Spring days of life. One from a powerful family or prestigious family background. Noble status and secure future. Now is the time to be fully happy with everything given. Lady of high status. Young lady.

26. STATE EXAMINATION

Many scholars are taking the state examination. Some of them dream of passing the examination in the first place, and some do of just passing the exam to at least become a low-ranked government official. The examinees writing down their answers look very serious. They compete to earn the opportunity to raise their family's social status and become their honor and pride. They would have to pull together all their knowledge and abilities if they are given a topic that they never anticipated. Back in those days, there were many who failed the exam multiple times over many years and never became a government official. On the other hand, some passed the exam at such a young age and held very important offices in their early twenties with their genius acknowledged.

Keywords

Will be taking an exam. Luck related to documents. Long-prepared things pan out in full-scale. No results yet, but the process is very important. Concentration required. This opportunity is dispositive. You will get homework that you must solve. Test ahead. Well-prepared.

27. PRISONER

A messy-haired man wearing a large wood cuff around his neck as punishment is locked up in the prison. There is a spilled rice bowl in front of him. He feels that the way he is being treated is unfair because he is not guilty. His intense, disobedient eyes seem to be saying that he has not given up. The guard, who apparently knows all of his story, looks a bit antsy. The prisoner could really be a man of very high status. During this period, those embroiled in factional strife, despite their innocence, were often imprisoned or sent on an exile. In the worst cases, they were executed but sometimes their false charges were removed and honor restored after death.

Keywords

Difficult but unexpected reversal awaits in the future. Meeting a very strong-willed, determined person. Frustrating situation where one cannot accomplish his/her objectives. Must not lose pride even in the midst of difficulties. Can get framed. For the time being, you will have a difficult time being heard out.

28. LAZY CROWN PRINCE

The crown prince, having great scholars as his teachers, is bored and tired of his daytime class. Furthermore, he even fell asleep and begins drooling after scribbling on his textbook; perhaps he is in food comma or just fooling around. The scholars with their obligation to teach the crown prince are embarrassed. They will get punished if they let the crown prince behave this way, but their days are just too long trying to teach the unruly crown prince. As the crown prince is not interested in academics and prefers outdoor activities, many books that he has to read to become a great king can be torturous. Of course, theory is not all there is for him to learn to become a great king, but to be able to manage his learned officials, he must not neglect to study.

Keywords

Meeting a young person with whom you cannot be so casual. For the time being, you have to maintain this relationship. Life with people with different stances. Cannot cry nor laugh. Not to the degree of a grave consequence, but still, bad habits will eventually lead to bad results. Immature person's rest.

29. COURT LADIES PAID SALARIES

Delighted court ladies are waiting in line for their turn to get paid for their salaries. The court attendants received their wages on a regular basis. They were loyal subjects to the king, but also enjoyed the satisfaction of accumulating wealth in exchange for their freedom. In some cases, they helped out their poor families outside the palace with this money. They also saved up for their retirement to prepare for their life outside the palace as they had to leave the palace when they became very old or ill. In times of severe drought or bad harvests a large number of court ladies would be asked to leave the palace as a ritual to pray for rain. But unless and until such thing happened, it was not possible for them to leave the palace even if they wished, so they had to prepare for their retirement on their own.

Keywords

Very practical happiness. Find satisfaction in small things. Benefit from trivial rather than from grand things. Joy found in one's own domain. Will discover something that is different from others. Wish comes true in everyday life. Small, realistic goal is accomplished faster than larger goals.

30. PRINCE AND PAUPER

It may just be a folktale, but could be based on a true story. The prince and the pauper, who looked identical to each other, crossed their paths one day and traded clothing, just for fun. What is going to happen as a result of this trading is unknown. The prince may never be able to return to his rightful position, or the poor boy may get in serious trouble if what he did is found out. Even the prince who lives a good life with nothing lacking wants to escape the suffocating palace life, and the beggar wants to escape his miserable life; both of them wish to change their fate even for a brief moment.

Keywords

Switched positions. Unexpected changes. Hanging out with people with unpredictable future. Very closely intertwined relationship, but very a dangerous gamble. Foolish acts. Must take responsibility for actions not so well thought out. Will make foolish choices to feel better.

31. PALACE PHARMACY

A palace physician and a nurse are making medicine. The dignified old physician is contently watching the nurse calmly brewing the medicine. The medicine sachets hanging from the ceiling and herbs are not for them, but for the royal family. The royal pharmacy was very strictly managed as it was a highly specialized area responsible for the health of the royal family. Even a slightest mistake could possibly make them lose their lives. Accordingly, the most skilled physicians and nurses of the time worked here. If any member of the royal family falls ill with a disease that even they could not cure, they had to take up on the task of finding and bringing in skilled physicians from outside the palace, tracking them down from mysterious hearsays about them. Anyhow, nothing bad was allowed to happen to the royal family because the royal physicians and nurses could not treat them.

Keywords

All problems (diseases) have a cure. Prepare for upcoming incidents in the ordinary times. Need to be prepared in various aspects. Requires expert knowledge. Will not only stop at knowledge, but will also highly develop skills in the areas of practical application. Demonstrate exceptional talents in service to others.

32. PALACE NURSE MAKING MEDICINE

A palace nurse is fanning the medicine brewer making medicine and another palace nurse with an ulterior motive is peeping from behind the door. The nurse brewing the medicine is so focused that she does not notice the other nurse behind her. Carefully managing the intensity of the charcoal fire to brew the medicine is such an important task that the nurse cannot take her eyes off the brewer even for a moment. She is constantly on top of the job, but human errors can be made at any time. If she lets her mind wander, the medicine can burn, so she has to stand by it at all times.

Keywords

Stay on top of it. A brief moment of carelessness may lead to a big problem. It takes a long time and great effort to succeed. But there is no guarantee that such devotion will necessarily bear fruits. But the mission must be accomplished and completed. Service for others. Or such an occupation.

33. PALACE LIBRARY

It is the royal library of the Joseon dynasty, a research institution for academics and public policies, and a totality of knowledge. It played a key role in the formulation of public policies and the preparation of materials to support the king's orders. There are bookshelves with many scrolls and books on them. The serious looking scholar working on some documents appears very determined and proud. Many achievements began here and were stored here for future generations. Therefore, the officials working here had to be very organized and intelligent. If the king suddenly ordered to locate a document, they had to move very quickly, and they also had to keep the place safe from fire.

Keywords

Achievements with small building blocks, or the integration of those building blocks; related to knowledge. Achievement is assessed based on intellect rather than by physical activities. Things will go nowhere unless you think deeply. May profit from work done by someone else. Auspicious luck in academics.

34. TORMENTED AND ANGUISHED

A court lady is sighing and looking at the carps in the pond in a quiet place of the palace. The seemingly middle-aged court lady entered the palace when she was very young. She laments as though her life confined in the palace is like that of the carps. The happy puppy next to her does not know any of this and is just being cute. The flowers on the trees in the distance are like the withering youth of the court lady. Her youthful years are now gone and she is counting the remaining days of her life in the palace. There is no way out of this but the life in the palace is too dull and boring to endure loneliness.

Keywords

Others would not know the meaning of the sigh. In one place with those who have completely different lives. Others cannot relate to my fears and worries. Frustration that cannot overcome the confined space. Agonize but back to square one. Banal worries of life. No change in life in the big picture. Lonely.

35. CORRUPT OFFICIAL

A greedy-looking official is on his way to the palace in a palanquin. The palanquin bearers look tired and unhappy. The fat official does not seem to know this and is only relaxed. From his attire he does not appear to be a very high ranking official, but he is all acting high and mighty as he feels elated that he earned his place. He would not let it slide if the palanquin bearers made even a very slight mistake. He might have happened to be lucky one day and bought his title with money. Although the social class system was rigid at the time, exceptions could always be made and there were quite a few who paid bribes to move up in the ladder. It was hard for the government to catch all such instances.

Keywords

Some chance of minor relocation. Not a big move but it can be a daunting task. May have to serve others or be served by others. Have to complete the task at hand now. Everyone has his or her role. Fated to accomplish the given task for the time being. But for not too long.

36. PALACE ATTENDANTS ON NIGHT WATCH

"Soonra" is keeping a night vigil where the court ladies and eunuchs walk through the hallways of the palace quarters holding lanterns. Soonra was carried out to prevent theft and fire and it was necessary to ensure that the same watching practice was carried out at night as well as during the day. The royal families could sleep comfortably at night knowing that they were well-protected. Even a single mistake could endanger the safety of the royal family. The palace structures were mostly built with wood so they were vulnerable to fire; once they caught fire, it was very difficult to put it out. Also, the royal family had to be careful of the dangers posed by the opposition and assassins sneaking in as the palace was a large place.

Keywords

Some matters require very close attention. Watch carefully and see if there is anything wrong in routinely performed matters. Peaceful time today was made possible by someone else's care and sacrifice. Protected by people you do not know. Remember that someone is looking out for you to cover all bases.

37. CONSPIRACY

Someone's hand is putting something in the medicine boiler. It is unknown if the added material is a medicinal ingredient to make the medicine more effective or if someone is intentionally putting in poison. Because there is no face shown, it is difficult to see exactly who is doing this and what this is. It is difficult to catch the conspirator, but even if you can guess, there is no evidence. In those days, it was inconceivable to perform an autopsy on the dead body of a royal family member, so the truth was often buried with the body. Therefore, there were many cases of conspiracy involving poisoning. The royal family was no exception to this. They were all the more vulnerable to such risk because they did not make their own food or medicine.

Keywords

Latent danger. Someone is out to slander or harm you. Need to be very cautious. If illness is the topic of the reading, not a good result. The one who made things happen is unknown. Be wary of the person nearest you. For now, you cannot tell who is going to harm you.

38. INCOGNITO KING

The king and his attendant in plain clothing are walking around in the marketplace. It is mid-winter and icicles are hanging at the end of the eaves. The king has a very serious look on his face as he is observing the lives of the commoners and the attendant is constantly on the lookout for the safety of the king. The king is wearing plain clothes but it is difficult to hide his noble status. The king seems to be shocked at witnessing the pain and suffering of his subjects contrasted with the splendid life of the palace. The young king who had never left the palace since birth, now realizes that the education he had received was not everything there was.

Keywords

Unfamiliar place. You have to temporarily play a different role. Learn unexpected knowledge or information. Temporary but necessary change. You need to know the underlying problem. Will get to see with your own eyes what you only have been hearing about. Information you only imagined in your mind finally becomes real.

39. KING'S CHIEF SECRETARY

The chief secretary who carries an order by the anguished king is leaving the chamber with a secret letter. It is probably a secret message from the king. The king seems to be in a situation where he cannot rely on anyone and has to make a lonely decision. The chief secretary hurriedly hits the road to carry out the royal command in a discreet manner. He looks determined to accomplish the objective of the high and lofty king in complete unison with the king. The king is in the highest position but for that reason he is not able to share his thoughts with those around him. Even with his wife, the queen, he had limits as to what he could share with her especially if she was from a family from a different political faction. Perhaps the chief secretary is only the one who truly understands the king's difficult position that is entangled with different interests.

Keywords

Getting things done in unison with one another. Helping hand extended in the midst of hardship. Will receive help from someone younger or socially inferior. Work executed in a discreet manner. Loyalty should be considered important. Gathering of people with very strong bonds that cannot be judged by simple interests. Or the progress of such people's work.

40. THE PRIME MINISTER

The prime minister is the highest ranking official just below the king and possesses all the honor and power. His gray beard and official garment display the dignity and spirit of an old veteran. The officials and court ladies passing by him pay respect to him, but he is looking away as though he is displeased at something. Of course, he can get almost whatever he wants. However, he constantly stays uptight in order to keep his enemies in check and remain where he is. This is probably same with the king, too – common to all powers.

Keywords

Peak time to enjoy everything. Excellent luck, but be careful not to be so conceited. Bright future down the road. Something will happen to make others respect you. Opportunity to brag and flaunt your status. Luck awaits to bring wealth and honor or equivalent. Firm power and position.

41. UNDERCOVER ROYAL INSPECTOR

The king spends most of his time in the palace, so it is difficult for him to know how his officials outside the palace are doing their job. Therefore, he occasionally sends an undercover royal inspector to catch them off guard and punish them for any wrongs that they have done. Even though the undercover inspector is wearing an ordinary scholar's clothes, the identification tag of a royal inspector shows under his clothes when the wind blows. A dog is roaring fiercely, blocking the inspector's path to the corrupt officials far away, who are drunk from their party. Even the dog looks greedy. They are two of a kind.

Keywords

Work being done without being revealed, or such a person. Spy. Espionage. No ordinary person who can be judged by his appearance. Result may seem delayed, but when it happens, it will happen faster than lightning. Brazen person who is socially inferior than you. Journey that requires you to complete your mission. Trustworthy person.

148

42. BRIBE

In this scene, those who smuggle various items into the palace are handing money to the guards at the palace gate. They appear cautious not to get caught so obviously they are not very proud of what they are doing. If they do get caught, the guard may get flogged. It is not clear what is loaded on the wagon, but likely those are not permitted items. It is true that at the palace any incoming items were strictly inspected, but after all, such inspections were performed by humans, and there were loopholes and mistakes that allowed illegitimate transactions like this to happen. Also, under the orders of higher-ups, outsiders could sneak in and out of the palace.

Keywords

Time for censorship and inspection. Strict, yet fairness is requested. Ulterior motives different from what shown on the surface. Secret deal made and kept hidden from other people. Black market. Nothing good comes out of being involved in illegality. Be careful not to get unintentionally caught up in illicit activities. Penny-wise, pound-foolish.

43. CHIEF EUNUCH

Even though he is only a eunuch, after having spent his youthful days in the turmoils of the palace, he is now the chief eunuch. He perhaps deserves this position. He has given up an ordinary life, accepted his fate, and has now become an integral part of the palace life. Since eunuchs were not able to have offsprings, they would adopt children and spend the rest of their lives relying on them. The chief eunuch is comfortably reclining in his seat and seems pleased getting a massage from a young eunuch.

Keywords

Can use a keen and tactful person. Best wits and tactfulness. But doubtful whether they will be faithful. Short, comfortable life after suffering. Cannot become the most powerful as there are still higher-ups in the hierarchy. Give one and take one. Unusual occupations.

44. CHIEF COURT LADY

Also known as the great chamber court lady, she is the head of all court ladies except the king's concubines and court ladies who have served the king in bed. The chief court lady was so powerful that she could even directly talk to the queen or the mother of the king, and she was intimately involved in the private affairs of the royal family. She had good authority as she was responsible for managing the palace household matters. The fierce chief court lady in the scene is scolding a young court lady who apparently broke a flower vase. It is not the young court lady's fault that the vase is broken. She may have been framed for what someone else – perhaps her subordinate – did. But for now, the young lady is only softly weeping.

Keywords

Will get reprimanded. Unavoidable, difficult situation. Being cornered and not knowing what to do. If you are a superior, you will have to reprimand your subordinate, and if you are a subordinate, you will be reprimanded by your superior. Can get humiliated for something you have not done.

45. COURT LADY "GRACED" BY KING

This is a case where a court lady serves the king in bed and is appointed as a "graced" court lady. The king could potentially sleep with any female in the palace from lowly female servants to court ladies. It was also the dream of all court ladies to drastically change their lives by being loved by the king. If a court lady serves the king in bed or even gives birth to the king's offspring, her status would be elevated suddenly, become a concubine and/or have her own gorgeous residence and ladies-in-waiting. However, such opportunity was rare. While there was only one king, there were as many as hundreds and thousands of court ladies, and each tried hard to be noticed by the king. Perhaps this could not be achieved by human efforts and was only made possible by divine favors.

Keywords

Meeting of people of different statuses. Confidential agreement. Great opportunity that will never come by again. You have to seize the once-in-lifetime opportunity; someone who is going to lift you up is coming into your life. Small faith will lead to great results. Gathering of people who cannot be judged by their appearance. Meeting of people with unexpectedly strong bonds.

46. FOOD TASTER COURT LADY

The food taster court lady was responsible for testing the king's food for poison by placing a silverware in the food. Sometimes, she would first taste the food and then serve it to the king. The king in the palace had to be on the constant watch for poison in his food. Slowly poisoning someone to death was a popular method of assasination at the time, so the role of the food taster court lady was very important. Many people were after the almighty king. They had a better chance of not getting caught by poisoning the king than forcibly taking the throne by revolting. As such, the king always had to closely monitor the activities of those potentially treacherous ones.

Keywords

Danger hidden in mundane life, or mission to discover such danger. Seemingly ordinary things that you nonetheless always have to be cautious about. Measure twice and cut once. Time for you to sacrifice yourself for others. Profession. Vocation. When in doubt, check and double check.

47. SECRET LOVE AFFAIR

Under the hazy moonlight, a court lady and a eunuch are having a secret love affair. Apparently they are meeting up in secret to avoid the eyes of other people. Many court attendants had to live a lonely life without a spouse, so often they fell for each other. The eunuch is expressing his affection by giving a gift of expensive jewelry to the court lady. If found out, he may have to pay for this with his life. Even though the laws of the palace were very strict, it was impossible to completely prevent the natural sentiment of love.

Keywords

Secret love affair. Love grows without realizing. Situation or relationship that cannot be known to others. Unexpected romance. Be careful, otherwise you will be humiliated big time. Secret should be forever kept as a secret.

48. SECRET DEAL

On a moonlit night, a senior court attendant is handing a letter to a young court lady. Their watchful eyes seem that they are involved in some sort of conspiracy. Or, of course, they may be taking this risk in order to deliver the message to their superiors. In any event, they would not avoid death if this leaked out. They would die either way – if they disobey the orders of their superiors or if the king finds out about this conspiracy. They had no choice but to fulfill their roles as a puppet in this strictly hierarchical system.

Keywords

Discharge your duties faithfully, but also consider the risk posed to you. Will be sharing a secret that others cannot find out about. Conspiracy and scheme. Can be easily discovered at this time, so take extra caution. Secret that will soon be revealed. Not a perfectly dependable person but must get along with him/her for the time being.

49. ROYAL MEAL TABLES

It was a palace custom for the court ladies to receive and eat leftover food on the royal meal tables when the king was done with his meal and retired the tables. This signified that whatever the king handed down was considered a gracious gift, and also that subordinates could only begin eating after the king was finished. The king was equated to a parent and because filial piety was based on respecting elders the king was respected as such. Of course, it was also a great pleasure from the court ladies to get to taste the fancy food on the royal meal tables. Since the king knew that the court ladies were waiting for the food, he deliberately and generously left behind a plenty of food for them. Having such delicious food could be the only joy of life for the court ladies.

Keywords

Unexpected gift, bonus. Implies luck or blessing flowing from top down. Will be endowed with many things by virtue of obedience. May win a small award or be honored. Will obtain a stable life by faithfully discharging your duties. Take advantage of the benefits of being around a competent person.

50. SUNDIAL

The sundial was invented to tell the time during the day when the sun was up on a clear day. The sundial was installed in a place of the royal palace where the sun shined brightly and it functioned to inform the time accurately within the palace. However, its function greatly diminished on a cloudy or rainy day. The court attendants informed the time not only to the people of the palace, but also to the people within the city walls, by striking a large bell in regular intervals. The time was announced in a slightly different format back then. The modern time is counted on an hourly basis, but at that time, the time of the day was announced based on twelve (12) time periods. Each period constituted a two-hour interval. For example, if you made a plan to meet someone at the "Ihn" hour, it meant any time between three (3) and five (5) o'clock in the morning. Were people used to this kind of waiting back then? What would it have been like for them?

Keywords

Things happen in an orderly manner. Nothing is reversed. No benefit if not done properly. Even small things have to proceed in order. Everything requires a deadline and process. Things, once gone, do not return. Will work on something that requires accuracy or meet someone of such character.

51. TUHO (ROYAL WINTER GAME)

Members of the royal family in silk clothing are cheerfully playing Tuho in the winter. Two teams throw arrows into the jar in front of them and the team that gets more arrows in the jar wins the game. A jar with ears is placed in the center of the courtyard, and the players throw arrows from about ten steps away from the jar; one arrow in the jar counts as one point. There was boredom even in the midst of what seemed to be a glamorous palace life and the palace folks played various games to find their own joy. The people in the scene look happy regardless of the outcome of the game. The distant mountains are covered with snow indicating that it is mid-winter now. The walls of the palace in the back seem to be protecting the royal family from outside dangers, but on the contrary, also symbolize their confined lives. Even for the royal family who had everything they ever wanted, joy came from small things.

Keywords

Seemingly a big deal but actually not that serious. Better to just focus on the game in front of you right now. It may turn out to be trivial. Extraordinary in the ordinary. Meaning in working together. Take some time off and relax. Your happiness is up to you.

52. YUTNORI, FOLK GAME

The court ladies are having fun playing Yutnori in their free time. Yutnori is a folk game played on the New Year's day by everyone regardless of their age and gender. The game is played for fun but it is said to carry the wish for a good harvest in the agricultural society. The game board symbolizes the farmland and the game pieces that proceed according to the Yut sticks thrown represent the change of seasons bringing a good harvest. In addition, the game board is also viewed as the constellations of the night sky. Since the court ladies were destined to stay within the palace, they had to find their own entertainment. Close court ladies often gathered together in small groups to have fun.

Keywords

Small happiness. You can have a peaceful time. Things that are not grand also have meaning. Relaxing time off. The more people involved in the activity, the better the efficiency and effectiveness. Wiser to let things go with flow than trying to find something great. They think they are better but comparison is meaningless. Just another group of mediocre people.

53. MISSING YOU

In contrast to the beautiful view of the green trees and the far away sky shown through the open window, tears are running on the face of the concubine who is holding a letter in her hand. It may be that some news arrived from her family outside the palace. Regardless of whether it is a happy or sad news, the thought that she is not able to see her family as often as she used to may have made her feel very sad. The process of becoming a member of the royal family must not have been so easy for her – having entered the palace at a young age when she still required the care of her family and learning the strict laws of the palace. Moreover, she was always lonely because she had no one to depend on. Even though she is fully adorned and clothed in gorgeous silk, she still cries missing her family outside the palace.

Keywords

News arrives. It may not necessarily be good news. However, some of the constraints are resolved. Faster results in private matters than in public matters. Luck is not against you, so it may be worthwhile to endure the hard times. You must play a role within the formalities. Limited freedom. Old nostalgia.

54. PERFORM ANCESTRAL RITES

Even the king and queen of the kingdom had to personally perform ancestral rites. Those with even the highest authority were no different from commoners in terms of the filial piety required of them. The basis of all things was filial piety and people were ruled with this principle. The ritual offerings are arranged in the ritual chamber with a view of the royal tomb. The tomb of the late king was placed at the same height as the throne when he was alive, and the current king was supposed to perform the ritual while looking at the scenery from the distant ritual chamber. The reason that the chamber was built at a certain distance is to show respect for the late king and to demonstrate the legitimacy and dignity of the dynasty to his officials and the subjects.

Keywords

Ceremony that happens only occasionally but must be performed. Will participate in a very important task. Rules and traditions must be followed. One's free will is not so important. Good luck follows from observing the superior's opinion. Will be obligated to serve senior members of the household at home or receive guests with hospitality.

55. ROYAL KITCHEN

Many court attendants are carrying around small dining tables. Some are preparing steaming hot dishes while others are busy making dumplings. Preparing meals for the king, Surasang, required a great amount of manpower. The most important part of the task was to provide a healthy meal to ensure the health of the king. As a result, fresh seafood and regional products were gathered from all over the country and used to prepare all sorts of seasonal delicacies. However, in times of drought or wars that devastated the lives of the common people, virtuous kings shared their subjects' pain and suffering by reducing the number of dishes on their meal tables. Of course, there were many other kings who died early of diabetes caused by gluttony. It is ironic that it is now known that coarse food is better for health.

Keywords

Feast is prepared. Will be invited to such a party or banquet. Or, will have to prepare a party or banquet for others. Can expect good news. However, may only have to prepare a feast for others, with no benefits to you. Busy workplace.

56. ROYAL GARMENT

The royal garment worn by the king is called Yongpo. It is made of yellow or red silk, and the Five Clawed Dragon (Ojoryong) embroidered with gold thread called Bo is sewn on the chest, back, and shoulders of the garment. There was a dedicated department that made clothes for the king, and there, specifically designated court attendants managed the finished clothes by ironing and adding scent to them. The court attendant holding an incense burner in the picture is adding the scent of incense to the royal robe. Yongpo symbolized the king's authority and was in fact considered as the king himself. It could only be worn by the one and only absolute power, so it had to be handled with exceptional care. The status of the royal family was identified with clothing. Among all of the royal clothing, of course, the garments of the king had to and did stand out the most. The colors of the royal garment changed slightly from time to time, but either yellow or red was used.

Keywords

Do not get your hopes up in matters in which you do not have a central role. If you are waiting for an outcome, it is premature now. Progress gets delayed and you stay passive. Cannot begin unless someone acts. Should not get going before the tide. Not much luck in moving. Things will take time and get delayed.

57. AMBASSADORS FROM MING

For the king, who had to maintain good foreign relations with the neighboring countries, foreign ambassadors were not easy guests to entertain. Foreign ambassadors occasionally visited the king for the purposes of advancing the interests of their own countries and the positions of their rulers. Therefore, they often acted arrogantly and took it for granted that they were received with the utmost courtesy. The ambassador getting off the palanquin and arrogantly looking at distant mountains is being greeted by a government official. With a displeased look on his face, he seems to have some trick up his sleeve. He is planning to greet the king and reveal his true motives soon. Clearly, of course, he is only planning to advance his country's own interests. If the king does not respond wisely, he would be forced to accept the ambassador's unreasonable demands for tributes, the burden of which will inevitably be passed onto his subjects.

Keywords

May have to take unpleasant orders from others. Unreasonable demands from far away. Will have to meet someone you cannot refuse or ignore. Scheduled meeting. The thief turns on the master with a club. Must be suppressed before it turns into a chain reaction. Have to be prepared for all scenarios. Even if you have covered all bases, you will meet someone who will make a surprising demand.

58. REGIONAL PRODUCTS

Regional products collected from all over the country are waiting to be inspected. Officials are meticulously going through their checklist and cross-checking the items. The royal family collected taxes in various items, such as linen, cotton or rice, but it was also very important to collect seasonal local products. Food products often went bad while in transportation in hot weather, so special care and attention was required. The royal family enjoyed the luxury of tasting all sorts of seasonal delicacies from all over the country, but the commoners had to bear all the hardship of bringing them to the royal tables. Thanks to their endeavors, the royal family could enjoy quality food and high culture, which eventually became our heritage and continued on to these days.

Keywords

Accumulation of wealth. Business thrives. Secure life with nothing lacking. Checks and inspections required. Bookkeeping or accounting requested. Manager of the wealth and property of another. Care and attention requested in traveling. Material abundance.

59. JOSEON MISSIONS TO JAPAN WEL-COMED

The ship dispatched from the kingdom of Joseon is anchoring in the Japanese port. The officer standing in the front deck of the ship is happy that they have finally arrived at their destination after a long sailing. A gentle breeze is blowing. Japanese noblemen are gathering in the port to see the envoys from Joseon. The people sent by the king of Joseon to the Japanese general had diverse backgrounds; much of cultural exchanges took place during this time. The purpose of the meeting was to resolve some urgent issues between the two countries or the affairs of the Japanese king alone, and the meeting had a profound influence on the culture of the royal family as well as the nobility. The Joseon mission brought to Japan a royal letter and gifts from their king to the Japanese king, and Japan welcomed them with the highest possible courtesy. Joseon missions visited Japan on twelve (12) occasions over two centuries since the 1600s. Their visits to Japan gave rise to many fascinating stories and stimulated various cultural exchanges throughout the entire country of Japan.

Keywords

Long-distance business trip or move. The farther away you go, the more benefits and honors you will be with. Good things happen in unfamiliar places. Time to encounter something new. Nothing good comes out of staying where you are. Duty to act on behalf of another person. Better luck in moving in groups.

60. RECEPTION FOR JOSEON MISSIONS TO JAPAN

The envoys are using their free time to recover from the long journey. They changed into comfortable clothes and apparently visited the mansion of some Japanese nobility. The insignia containing the Japanese shogunate coat of arm hanging as a backdrop suggests that the host is a very high-class official. There are authentic Japanese sashimi dishes and sake on the table. The envoys put on a big smile as they enjoy the night in a foreign country. During this period, Joseon and Japan had a friendly relationship, so the visits were not limited just to formalities. People of the two countries engaged in in-depth cultural exchangs and they understood and respected their differences. In addition, the benefits that both countries gained from these experiences contributed to their development and progress at all levels.

Keywords

Will serve a very important guest or be received as an important guest. Unusual experience. Will encounter unknown but good luck. Will interact with foreigners. Will encounter new things. Take time off. After hard work, you are allowed to take some rest in luxury. WIll interact with classy people. Travel that enriches your experience.

61. FALLING BLOSSOMS ON FLOWING STREAM

The concubine is looking at the flower petals falling into the pond in the courtyard of the palace. She apparently does not know that her youth is more beautiful than the flowers. Or, she may be thinking about something else without looking at the flowers. This card has a different meaning from the one in which an old court lady is watching the carps in the pond and lamenting. A concubine, as the king's woman, had everything, except perhaps freedom, and if she was lucky, she could even become the queen. Although on some occasions a court lady was elevated to the status of a concubine upon serving the king in bed, such a case was very rare. Only beautiful, talented young ladies from prestigious families could become concubines; they were selected and appointed when the queen did not give birth to a son or there were some other reasons. In any event, it is a beautiful time of her life.

Keywords

Unrealized happiness. Your complaints are blessings to others. Already given happiness and destiny. Temporary deviation. Be aware of people's attention. Be careful not to become a topic of other people's gossip. Do not tell others about your happiness or misfortunes. Will be placed in an enviable position without knowing.

62. TURTLE SHIP

Constructed by Admiral Yi Sun-Shin right before the Japanese invasion of the Imjin War, the Turtle Ship inflicted heavy damage on the Japanese military. It is considered the world's first assault-armored ship. Even as the lightning strikes the sea, the Turtle Ship is rushing forward without hesitation, displaying its fearless spirit. Inspired by the shape of a sea turtle, a mystical sea creature, the unique form of the ship not seen anywhere else in the world is very impressive. Since Korea is surrounded by the sea on three sides, it has had strong maritime traditions. Koreans were highly adept at naval battles, proudly maneuvering through the paths of the ocean like a sea turtle. The wind waves are rising in the complete darkness. However, the ship is proceeding with the turtle's uncrushable face facing forward. Of course, even more courageous generals and soldiers must be rowing on board on the inside.

Keywords

Can see what is not shown. Mystical abilities. Will suffer a loss if you continue to stay where you are. It takes great courage to reverse the crisis. Good judgment required. Many changes amidst frequent relocations. Do not listen to what other people say; stick to your own beliefs. Courageous spirit that will not be controlled by the surroundings.

63. JAGYEOKRU (WATER CLOCK)

This water clock was invented by Jang Yeong-sil under the order of King Sejong. It is a device designed to inform the time by having three (3) dolls strike the bell, drum and gong when the water is filled up to a certain level. In the picture, an official is tuning it to enhance the accuracy of the time. The function of the clock was not only to accurately tell the time, but also to properly measure the seasons of the year. Knowing the seasons was closely related to the success of agriculture, and at that time, agriculture was a very important matter that could control the fate of a country. Furthermore, the support of the king was necessary for the research and development of practical science and technology. During the reign of a wise king, culture and technology prospered, and talented people could step forward and contribute their skills.

Keywords

Requires practical skills, not just theories. Good results expected if you choose such a job. Academic, theoretical discussions are meaningless. Support from an influential person. Better results expected if the matter is widely known. More benefits from acting for a bigger cause than for a small purpose.

64. METAL MOVABLE TYPE

The Korean Buddhist text printed with the world's first metal movable type (printed during the Goryeo dynasty, 78 years earlier than Gutenberg's), Jikjishimchaeyojul (Anthology of Great Buddhist Priests), is abbreviated as Jikji. The text was purchased by a man named Collin de Plancy, the first French ambassador to Korea at the end of the Korean Empire in the late 19th century, and the book eventually ended up in the National Library of France after changing hands several times. Dr. Byung-Sun Park later discovered the book in the library while he was working as a librarian there. Afterwards, this book became the first and only UNESCO-designated Memory of the World Programme not located in its originating country. The invention of metal types had a profound effect on human history as it was a revolutionary turning point that dramatically advanced the culture of the mankind. Prior to that, the mankind transferred knowledge by manually copying manuscripts onto parchment paper. The master printer in the picture is anxiously trying to print another text with the metal type.

Keywords

Media or widely reproduced rumors or information. The more standardized the task, the more it suits one's aptitude. Rewarding results originate from small ideas. Begins with a small idea. Occupation dedicated to serving others. Fulfilling such a role would be meaningful. Information kept only to yourself is not fun.

171

65. TREASON

Kings always feared treason. Treason was committed by or on behalf of the king's siblings of similar rank, another member of the royal family, or the one involved in the interests of many others. Overthrows were attempted in many different ways and some actually succeeded and even ascended onto the throne. Most, if not all, of the ousted kings had to face a miserable ending. The kingship was known to be mandated by heaven but in reality political power struggles were ruthless beyond imagination even to the extent that many involved in such struggles ultimately abandoned to follow the human and/or moral laws. The dark atmosphere created by the warriors gathered up holding torches at night seems to demonstrate the calm before the storm. Nobody can tell whether their conspiracy will succeed. To them, their success in the imminent rebellion is the only thing that matters now.

Keywords

Cannot clearly tell right from wrong because you are trapped in your own thoughts. Temperance is required because the objectives and targets are unclear. Be cautious of working with people who are rushing. In low-ranking position, have no decision-making authority; in high-ranking position, will need to take responsibility for the thing that is being done now. Very risky venture.

66. ROYAL SEAL

The royal seal is the official stamp of the state made of jade. It symbolizes the national sovereignty and the king himself, and was used in official government documents. The orders of the king were hardly retracted once they were officially issued. As such, the king needed to exercise his discretion prudently, and any documents stamped with the royal seal had to be executed the way that they were issued. Many families kept the official documents handed down to them by the king as heirlooms, and in the modern times, they have great cultural values. The royal seal taken away was analogous to getting the throne taken away. As the ruler's authority depended on how much of his commands were actually executed, the royal seal symbolized his power to make things happen. It is said that in the midst of many wars the royal seal was stolen several times. The royal seal is indeed a valuable item that shared the fate of the kingdom.

Keywords

Approval needed from a very high-level organization. Work delayed due to formality. Takes time to get results. Communication is delayed. If you are in a position of waiting for orders, you will remain passive, and on the contrary, if you are in a position to make a decision, you will no longer be able to just sit and wait. Formal procedure.

67. CONCUBINE PUTTING ON MAKEUP

The lady member of the royal family gets up and adorns herself every morning. She is looking in the mirror and trying to put on some trendy makeup. Things are not that much different from these days. Even in those old days, women used various makeup tools, including rare items imported from abroad, to enhance their beauty, as well as a secret folk method known to be effective. The fact that some women used mercury, the toxic effect of which was not known at the time, to make their faces look pale, evidences their strong desire for beauty. Female members of some of the most well-off, powerful families at the time tried very hard to keep their youthful looks. Reportedly, the government implemented laws and regulations to curtail these women's excessive indulgence in extravagance. Although the concubine in the picture looks beautiful enough even without her makeup on, she cannot take her eyes off of the mirror.

Keywords

Too much is as bad as too little. Excessive can be worse than insufficient. You do not see what is around you because you are too focused on yourself. Narcissism. Excessive narcissism can ruin everything. Paying too much attention to what others would think, you no longer know what you truly need. Will get a job that requires you to reveal yourself in front of others.

68. HYANGWONJEONG (PALACE BUILDING)

This pavilion is a palace structure used as a rest area for the king and his family in the late Joseon dynasty. This building has a very high historical, artistic, and architectural value in that the space creates a sense of proportion with hexagonal cornerstones and surface, and a hexagonal roof. It is a small, but well-balanced structure. The autumn leaves are falling onto the pond in front of it and the sky is filled with exquisite shades of the sunset. Even the king who possessed the entire world did not need a large space for his break. The building was built with the understanding of exactly how much space a person would need to feel cozy and comfortable in it.

Keywords

Resting place. Relaxed in peace. Even though you are not the main character, you are satisfied with your supporting role. Give yourself a break. Get away to a quiet place. Need some secret space. Have to know that you already have everything.

69. KYEONGHOERU (PALACE BUILDING)

Kyeonghoeru, described as the most beautiful place in the palace and analogized to a flower, was built during the reign of King Taejong. In the view that the west side of the Kyeongbokgung Palace was a wetland, a large pond was dug there and a pavilion was built on top of it. A foreign ambassador, impressed with the spectacular view, wrote about the place as follows: the dragon and flowers carved into the stone pillars of the pavilion reflected on the water made it look as if a dragon was swimming in the water. The name of the pavilion has a special meaning. As the first virtue of the king, regardless of how powerful and able he was himself, was to attract talents, the word Kyeonghoe means the virtuous meetings of the king and his officials. Kyeonghoeru was a great place to hold royal banquets to celebrate happy occasions, but this was also a place where King Danjong was tragically forced to hand over his royal seal to his ruthless uncle King Sejo and where the ousted former king Yeonsan-gun had instituted Heungcheong (a department dedicated to recruiting beautiful women for the king) before he was dethroned, which later became the origin of the word Heungcheong-mangcheong (roughly meaning squandering).

Keywords

Can enjoy many good things, but if not careful, you can fall into debauchery. The job involves the construction of an overall structure with authority and dignity, so it is suitable for public work. There will be serious consequences if you abuse a given opportunity. Take advantage of the opportunity to stand in front of other people. Will win some big award or be congratulated.

70. KEUNJEONGJEON (PALACE BUILDING)

It is the central building standing in Kyeongbokgung Palace, where coronations, royal weddings and other state ceremonies were held, and symbolizes the royal family of Joseon. With all very important official ceremonies and rituals having been performed here, this place constitutes the face and essence of the palace. Keunjeong means diligent governance. Diligence was one of the highly valued virtues of the king in governing the country. The king was supposed to diligently work to put the comfort of his subjects ahead of his own and his enjoyment of the power. In addition, in Keunjeongjeon, official functions, such as banquets and fireworks for foreign ambassadors, were carried out. The structure was built with eye-catching splendors to exhibit the pride of the kingdom. Most national events that needed to demonstrate the magnificence of the kingdom reportedly took place here.

Keywords

Essence of all things. Symbolizes the central figure. Favorable in formal matters but not very helpful in private matters. Favorable in making progress within an organization or a system. Advantageous to have a big event. Time to perform to show work results to the outside. Will attract the attention of other people.

71. CHANGKYEONGGUNG (PALACE BUILD-ING)

Changkyeonggung Palace was constructed by King Sejong for his father King Taejong, and was originally called Suganggung, meaning a long life in peace. After some time had passed, the palace was renovated as a residence for the king's mother and queen dowagers and was renamed Changkyeonggung, meaning prosperity and joyfulness. Therefore this palace is not very closely connected to national politics. Rather, the palace is known for its beautiful harmony with the nature. A stream called Okryucheon flows in front of Honghwamun, the main gate of the palace, and the water is called Myeong-dangsu, meaning that the water carries auspicious energy from the mountains and rivers. During the Japanese colonial period, this palace suffered the humiliation of being converted into a zoo but its status was restored and it once again displays its graceful beauty.

Keywords

Turning point. Opportunity to restore wealth and honor. Can enjoy blessings and good wealth without much difficulty. Stable life under protection. Good time to retire if you plan on retiring. Activities may be limited. Not auspicious in long journeys or long-distance business trips.

72. INJEONGJEON (PALACE BUILDING)

It is another part of the palace for King Taejong and the name of the building means benevolent governance. A phoenix symbolizing a peaceful and prosperous era is painted on the inside walls of the building. Before he ascended to the throne, Taejong Lee Bang-won (King Taejong) purged a large number of people in bloodbath including many officials who were loyal to the previous dynasty. Later, the country was stabilized and an era of peace began, and his son, King Sejong, became known as the greatest king of the Joseon dynasty. King Taejong, thinking about the decisions he had to make in the past, may have decided to rule with benevolence in the new era to come. The Joseon dynasty continued on for the next 500 years. Most, if not all, of the foundations for the new country were laid out during this time and as was intended by the king. This is the place where the coronation ceremonies for several Joseon kings were performed. Official functions of the kingdom, such as welcoming receptions for foreign ambassadors, were carried out here as well. This picture of the early spring with flower petals floating in the wind seems to depict the history and dreams of the palace.

Keywords

Finding a solution after a big conflict. Change in the circumstance. Positive changes coming up. The first part of the work is completed; you now have to think about the next step. You may proceed as planned. WIll have good luck in official matters. Will receive an official recognition or be selected for a public post.

73. MOON JAR 1

The officers from the palace under the order of the king are hanging outside to request something. This is a kiln where high-quality ceramics are manufactured. The craftsman does not even notice that the officers have arrived outside as he is so preoccupied with examining the clay out of which he will make potteries. Quality raw material was essential to producing good porcelains and next in importance was the temperature of the fire. These experts were very valued as the process of pottery-making was not standardized and the craftsmanship completely depended on the skills of those craftsmen. They also took much pride in their work as they passed on their secret techniques from the master to the apprentice. It is probably the spring time as the petals are floating in the wind.

Keywords

Must focus on the basics of worldly matters. Pointless to skip a step. Such would likely lead to going around in circles. Good to follow traditions. Unexpected guests or offers. Such offers are not bad. Good enough, acceptable conditions.

74. MOON JAR 2

The officers are casting a doubtful eye over the shoulders of the craftsman who is diligently spinning the wheel and making pottery. But, of course, the craftsman's mind is completely fixed on the pottery. He is working on the very important step of the pottery-making process in which he is solely relying on the sensations of his hand to shape the porcelain. Even briefly losing his breath can ruin the whole thing. The way he is creating the porcelain with such tender care is similar to a person's life. It is similar in that whether the life of a person would turn out to be a great masterpiece or just a mediocre product depends on who is leading and/or making it. It may seem that a person can change his or her own destiny but sometimes life takes unexpected turns with other people's interventions.

Keywords

Steps that require blood, sweats and tears. Wandering mind will ruin the work. Have one thing completed and then move on to the next. Eagerness alone will not get the job done. Will win the battle against yourself. Honing your skills before competition. Has to be work you can understand on your own.

75. MOON JAR 3

Now, the craftsman puts the porcelain in the kiln and makes a fire. The temperature of the kiln differs all throughout the four seasons, and it is adjusted solely by the skills of the craftsman. The red flames of the kiln seem to represent the craftsman's passion. In no time, fresh green is lush outside. The summer time is in bloom. Not minding the heat, the craftsman is replenishing the fire. The kiln has to reach the right temperature to produce porcelains of desired quality. Now the time will do the rest. Nevertheless, the craftsman is not leaving the kiln as if he is waiting for the birth of his child.

Keywords

Patience and endurance through a dull and boring period. But the wait is not meaningless. Will soon obtain visible results. Inauspicious to move. Heart and passion for one goal. Now or never. Job may not involve dealing with people. Must put in wholehearted efforts and devotion.

76. MOON JAR 4

After the kiln cools down, the craftsman takes out the porcelains and checks them one by one with an eye of a hawk. He is meticulously examining them to see whether there are any flaws that will prevent them from being tagged as a masterpiece, such as fine cracks or air bubbles. Each and every one of the porcelains is like his child. However, he would be very disappointed if there were any porcelains that do not muster his standard. In any event, he is making an extraordinary effort to examine all the porcelains one by one. In fact, it was not likely that only a portion of the porcelains from one particular kiln would have defects; if one of them was no good, then the chances are that the rest of them were all likely to be the same because the raw material, as well as the temperature of the kiln, was same for all of them.

Keywords

Do work that makes you feel proud. Truth that cannot be compromised. If you desire high honors, be prudent in your judgment. Be honest and fair to yourself. Otherwise, you will regret it later. Outstanding skills in technical matters. Trust your judgment.

77. MOON JAR 5

The craftsman is destroying all the porcelains that are not up to his standard. He only wants to cry. His arduous endeavor was wasted down the drain. The officers who came by to see the progress are whispering to each other feeling sorry for him. But the craftsman is more heartbroken than anyone else. Apparently he never anticipated that this would happen to the porcelains to which he extended a great amount of care and effort as if they were his children. No matter how hard you try, there is always what-ifs. Every time he produced his work, he must have felt the same. The craftsman never put any imperfect porcelains out on the market. That was a matter of his reputation and honor. The season is now autumn.

Keywords

Requires a bold decision. Will fail if you hesitate now. Must not pass initiatives onto others. Have to finish what you started. Have to solve the problems you created yourself. Overcome your difficulties with a strong will. Don't worry about what others would think. Help from others will only hinder you now.

78. MOON JAR 6

The perservering craftsman once again spins the wheel and makes porcelains. He looks all the more resolved. Outside, the officers who came to wait for the product are now so tired that they start dozing off to sleep. Enough time has elapsed to fill the frontyard with autumn leaves. The officers are complaining and pressing the craftsman but he does not hearing anything anymore. He is in a battle against himself making the porcelains. He has no interest in knowing what is going on in the world or what season it is now. Perhaps this is the only way a perfect porcelain can be produced.

Keywords

Will reach the quintessence of the work. Everything is ripe. Subjectives and objectives united into one. Have to be immersed in your own world. Will win the lonely fight. Seemingly ordinary everyday life, but an extraordinary day that only you would know. Great responsibility. Professionalism. Hard life.

185

79. MOON JAR 7

The craftsman is now replenishing the fire for the second time. His face reflected in the flames is like the face of an enlightened guru. He is now only praying to the heaven that the porcelains, into which he had put so much effort, will turn out well. He probably has done all he could. Perhaps he is reminiscing the past watching the flames. Could he be thinking that a completed porcelain turns into a true masterpiece only through resignation, just as how it works in life? Next to him, the exhausted officers tired from waiting fell asleep and are even snoring.

Keywords

Results are coming soon. Darkest right before the sun rises. What everyone has forgotten about is revived. Second attempt is rather more effective. Good things will happen if you do not rush. The longer you endeavor, the more successful you will be.

80. MOON JAR 8

He finally got the Moon Jar he wanted. The craftsman is overwhelmed with joy, holding the porcelain out to the officials in satisfaction. The officers who have just woken up can hardly believe that the work finally succeeded after a long wait. Icicles are hanging on the eaves of the roof and it is now the winter, but the finally completed work makes the people totally forget about their long, difficult wait. A masterpiece came after a long journey. The is a reminder of the simple truth that nothing is gained for free. It is all the more precious because it is not easily obtainable.

Keywords

Completion. Finally obtain the desired result. Second attempt will be successful without fail. Long-awaited wishes come true. Technical completion. Now at the level of a master. Unusual beauty. Nobleness that ordinary people cannot appreciate. Satisfying results continue inside and out in a series.

81. MOON JAR 9

The finally completed Moon Jar is presented to the king. The king wants to bring in and reward the craftsman who produced this great porcelain with praises for his hard work and gold and silver treasures. The king's pleased expression indicates that he has a very fine taste in aesthetics. At the time the ability to produce beautiful, high-quality porcelains greatly enhanced the national dignity, so wise kings supported and helped nurture various areas besides politics. In particular, this plain-looking jar, without any patterns or decorations, is no ordinary porcelain. The mouth of the jar being much wider than the bottom creates a sense that the jar is floating in the air. This elicits an imagination of the moon floating above the thatched roof descending into the heart of the mind.

Keywords

Receiving an award or recognition at a big function. Pass through the last hurdle. The harder the exam, the better luck in the result of the exam. Will excel in the realm of seemingly impossible. Receive an unexpected gift or unexpectedly meet a person who will be of great help to you. Honor coupled with wealth coming to you.

82. MOON JAR 10

This fine Moon Jar is now displayed in the corner of the palace and foreign ambassadors and guests visiting the palace can appreciate its beauty. Of course, to more important guests, the porcelain could also be given as a gift. The Moon Jar has a subtle and mysterious luster and with its center slightly twisted, the intended asymmetry adds more to its beauty. Koreans make a wish upon the full moon; naturally they created a porcelain that resembled the full moon. For everyone, both the king and the commoners alike, the future is uncertain and unforeseeable. Paradoxically, however, this masterpiece was created out of the desire to find wisdom and beauty even among such unpredictable life. The world view of the Korean people is condensed in this Moon Jar.

Keywords

Receive recognition in a bigger world. Beneficial to be widely known. Time to express and share your thoughts that you used to keep to yourself. Unfavorable if narrow-minded. Think with wide lattitude. You are evaluated by others but will eventually gain good results. Must not judge by appearance.

리딩 방법 및 예제

Reading and Example

38. INCOGNITO KING

41. UNDERCOVER ROYAL INSPECTOR

47. SECRET LOVE AFFAIR

56. ROYAL GARMENT

1.이동운은 그림속 주인공의 움직임 여부로 알아
볼 수 있다.
· 변복한 왕, 암행어사, 조선통신사

2.그림속의 배경은 계절, 낮과 밤도 골고루 묘사
되어 있으므로 질문의 시기와 시간적 흐름을 알
아볼 수 있다.
· 향원정, 근정전, 달항아리 8 등

3.사람이 등장하지 않고 사물(물건이나 건물 등)
이 묘사된 것은 질문자 본인의 역량보다도 주변의
여건이나 객관적인 상황을 말해주는 것이 좋다.
· 경회루, 창경궁, 거북선 등

4.질문자가 궁금해 하는 인물을 추측할 때에는 그
림속 주인공의 연령대로 추측한다.
· 대왕대비, 세자의 술래잡기, 수놓는 공주 등

5.인물의 지위가 높고 낮음에 따라 중요도를 판
단한다.
· 대표석으로 왕족과 궁인들

6.그림속 인물들의 생활상을 보면서 어느 정도의
긴박함이 있는지를 파악한다.
· 사냥하는 왕, 역모 등 - 매우긴박
· 게으른 세자 - 시간이 지체됨

7.그림속에 결과가 도출되지 않고 과정만 묘사되
면 질문자의 해답 역시도 결과물이 나오지 않는
다.
· 옥새, 달항아리 9 등 - 결과물이 나옴
· 밀회, 스파이 등 - 결과물을 아직 모름

193

38. INCOGNITO KING

41. UNDERCOVER ROYAL INSPECTOR

47. SECRET LOVE AFFAIR

56. ROYAL GARMENT

1. Querent's luck in moving or relocation can be read from the characters' movements.

· Incognito King, Undercover Royal Inspector, Joseon Missions to Japan, etc.

2. Background images depict different seasons and day and night, enabling reading of the timing and chronological flows of the questions.

· Hyangwonjeong, Keunjeongjeon, Moon Jar 8, etc.

3. Where images depict no people but things (objects and buildings, etc.), focus should be on external factors or objective situations rather than Querent's own capabilities.

· Kyeonghoeru, Changkyeonggung Palace, Turtle Ship, etc.

4. Age of Querent's subject can be surmised from the age of the character(s).

· Queen Dowager, Prince Playing Tag, Embroidery by Princess, etc.

5. Degree of importance can be read from the rank and status of the character(s)

· Royal family and court attendants

6. Degree of urgency can be read from the situations the character(s) is/are in.

· King's Hunting, Treason, etc. – Very Urgent

· Lazy Crown Prince – Time Delayed

7. Where images depict only process and not any product, there is no real result in Querent's matter, either.

· Royal Seal, Moon Jar 9 – There is product

· Secret Love Affairs, Spy – No product

Question 다음 달에 출장을 가는 것이 좋을까요?

▼

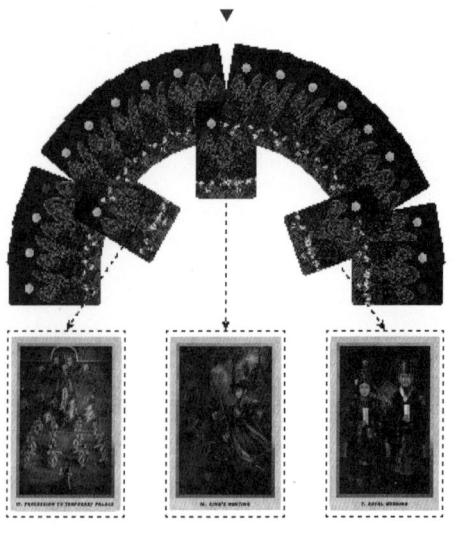

- Tip -

자신이 선호하는 방식으로 배열하셔도 됩니다.

시간 순서와 흐름에 따른 리딩 **Reading**

▼

행차: 최근 잦은 이동운이 들어와 있기 때문에 출장을 가는 것이 좋을 것 같고, 지금은 이동을 해야지 만족한 결과를 맺을 수 있습니다.

사냥하는 왕: 하지만 출장을 가게 된다면 객지에서 의외의 복병이 있을 수 있기 때문에 만반의 준비를 해서 가야만 하겠습니다.

왕가의 결혼: 일을 잘 마치고 돌아오게 된다면 좋은 결과가 기다리고 있으며 계약 등이 성사가 되겠습니다.

자신만의 리딩을 완성해보세요. **Practice**

첫 번째 카드 **행차:** 질문의 원인
두 번째 카드 **사냥하는 왕:** 질문의 결과
세 번째 카드 **왕가의 결혼:** 질문의 키워드

- Tip -

*키워드란 질문의 해결을 위한 **열쇠**같은 역할.*
원인과 결과, 키워드를 잘 조합하여 연습해보세요.

Question: Should I go on a business trip next month?

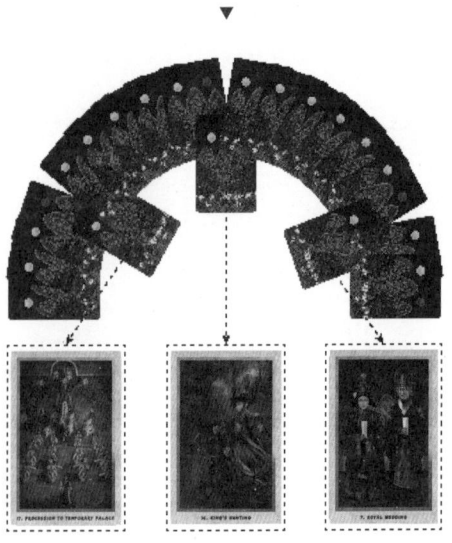

- Tip -
Cards can be spread as you like.

Reading: Reading according to chronological order and flow.

▼

Procession to Temporary Palace: Luck in movement is in. Querent should go on the business trip. He/she has to move around now to garner satisfactory results.

King's Hunting: But on the business trip, Querent may face an unexpected ambush, so Querent should be well-prepared before departure.

Royal Wedding: Good results will await Querent after returning from the trip; business transaction(s) will be entered into/consummated.

Completel your own reading.   **Practice**

▼

First Card: Cause of the Matter.
Second Card: Effect (Result) of the Matter.
Third Card: Keyword of the Matter.

- Tip -
*Keyword provides a solution to the question like the **key**.*
Practice reading with Cause, Effect(Result) and Keyword.

Question 계약이 성사가 된다면 이익을 보는 시기는?

▼

- Tip -

세컨드 카드를 뽑아 그 시기를 짐작할 수 있습니다.

카드 배경의 계절/시간으로 리딩　**Reading**

▼

달항아리 8: 계약이 성사되는 시기는 아마도 가을이 지나서 겨울쯤이 될 듯합니다. 또한 결과가 굉장히 좋을 수 있겠습니다.

> 질문자가 추가로 질문을 한 경우, 세컨드 카드를 1~2장 뽑아 카드 배경의 계절에 따라 그 시기를 짐작할 수 있습니다.
>
> 만약 세컨드 카드가 [달항아리 5]라면 시기는 늦여름이 지나 가을이 시작되는 쯤이며 이익을 보기에는 힘든 상황이라고 리딩 하시면 됩니다. 하지만 이것은 단편적인 설명이며 질문자의 상황에 따라 키워드에 맞는 리딩을 하시면 됩니다.

계절이 잘 표현되어있는 카드　**Point**

▼

봄 : 태실, 종묘, 공주의 술래잡기, 달항아리 2..
여름 : 사냥하는 왕, 해시계, 경회루..
가을 : 왕비의 산책, 세자의 술래잡기, 향원정..
겨울 : 석고대죄, 왕의 변복, 투호, 달항아리 8..

- Tip -

계절, 낮과 밤이 표현되지 않은 카드가 나올 경우
카드가 처해진 상황을 설명하면 된다.

Question: If a business transaction is entered into and/or consummated, when will Querent start making profit?

▼

80. MOON JAR 8

- Tip -
Read timing by picking a secondary card.

Reading: Read based on the card's season and/or time of the day.

▼

Moon Jar 8: Transaction will probably be consummated around in the winter past fall. Also, the results will be excellent.

If Querent asks an additional question, pick 1 or 2 secondary cards and read timing based on the seasons depicted in the cards.

If the secondary card is Moon Jar 5, the time will be around the beginning of the fall past summer and Querent will not see much profit. However, this is just one dimension of the explanation and you may conduct reading based on keywords in accordance with Querent's specific situations.

Cards with well-depicted seasons.　　**Point**

Spring: Royal Placenta Chamber, Play Blindfold Tag, Moon Jar 2...

Summer: King's Hunting, Sundial, Kyeonghoeru...

Fall: Queen Taking Stroll, Prince Playing Tag, Hyangwonjeong...

Winter: Asking for Forgiveness, Incognito King, Tuho, Moon Jar 8...

- Tip -

If the card does not depict seasons or day or night, explain the situation(s) depicted in the card.

Question 약혼자가 결혼을 미룬다. 무슨 이유일까?

▼

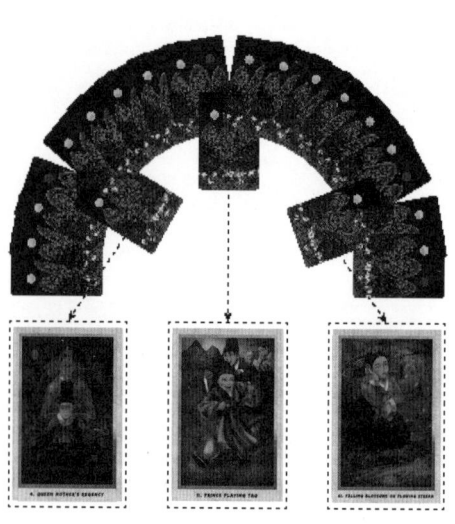

- Tip -
카드를 3장 이상 뽑으면 그만큼 리딩이 풍부해집니다.

204

인물의 영향력으로 카드를 리딩 **Reading**

▼

수렴청정: 결혼을 약속한 상대방의 부모님이나 허락을 받아야 하는 나이드신 분이 계신 듯 합니다. 그분의 뜻대로 움직여야 하는 상황일 수 있겠네요.

술래잡기(공주/세자): 게다가 본인이 어떻게 해야 할지도 지금 막막합니다. 너무 낙관적인 성격일 수도 있고 철이 없기도 하구요.

낙화유수: 그러다보니 시간만 보내고 지금은 딱히 이렇다 할 결론이 나질 않는 상황이네요. 주도적으로 일을 진행하기 어려우니 기다리는 것이 좋겠습니다.

자신만의 리딩을 완성해보세요. **Practice**

첫번 째 카드 **수렴청정** : 질문의 원인
두번 째 카드 **술래잡기** : 질문의 결과
세번 째 카드 **낙화유수** : 질문의 키워드

- **Tip** -

키워드란 질문의 해결을 위한 **열쇠**같은 역할.
원인과 결과, 키워드를 잘 조합하여 연습해보세요.

205

Question: Querent's finance is postponing the wedding. What is going on?

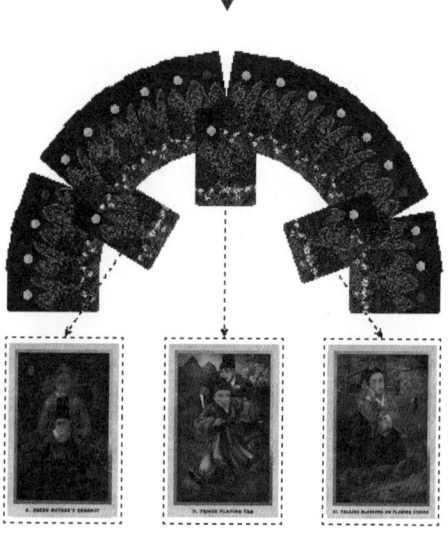

- Tip -
Pick 3 or more cards for better storytelling of the reading.

Reading: Read based on the influencial power of the character(s).

▼

Queen Mother's Regency: Fiance apparently needs a permission from his/her parents or another older member of the family. It may be that fiance must follow their will.

Playing Tag (Princess/Prince): He/she does not know what to do him/herself. He/she could be optimistic or immature.

Falling Blossoms on Flowing Stream: At this time, only the clock is ticking and there is no answer. Difficult to take an initiative and lead the situation. Better to wait for now.

Complete your own reading. ***Practice***

▼

First Card: Cause of the Matter.
Second Card: Effect (Result) of the Matter.
Third Card: Keyword of the Matter.

- Tip -
*Keyword provides a solution to the question like the **key**.*
Practice reading with Cause, Effect(Result) and Keyword.